Color for impact

Jan V. White
BookSmiths, Inc

Also by Jan V. White

Graphic Idea Notebook (2nd edition, Rockport Publishers, Rockport, MA, 1991)

Color for the Electronic Age (Watson-Guptill, Xerox Press, New York, 1990)

Graphic Design for the Electronic Age (Watson-Guptill, Xerox Press, New York, 1989)

Great Pages (Serif Publishing, Xerox, El Segundo, CA, 1990)

Xerox Publishing Standards, *co-author* (Watson-Guptill, Xerox Press, New York, 1988)

The Grid Book (Letraset USA, Paramus, NJ, 1987)

Using Charts and Graphs (R.R.Bowker, New Providence, NJ, 1984)

Mastering Graphics (R.R.Bowker, New Providence, NJ, 1983)

Designing for Magazines (2nd edition, R.R.Bowker, New Providence, NJ, 1982)

Editing by Design (2nd edition, R.R.Bowker, New Providence, NJ, 1982)

18 Ready-to-use Grids (National Composition Association, Arlington, VA, 1980)

On Graphics: Tips for Editors (Ragan Communications, Chicago, 1980)

Learn Graphic Design *video* (VideoTutor, Austin, TX 1989)

Printed in the United States of America. First printing, September 1996.

ISBN 9624891-9-0

Published by:
Strathmoor Press, Inc.
2550 Ninth Street, Suite 1040
Berkeley, California 94710-2516
Order toll-free (800) 217-7377
E-mail info@strathmoor.com

Getting the best out of color

Color makes everything look better: it creates a richer image, more powerful advertising, more captivating presentations. Color leverages the power of the first impression. It is intuitive and we all understand it, so we must use it as a tool for communication.

Raises perception of quality: both printed matter and presentations were voted* 60% better if they were in color. The decision whether to pay attention or throw the publication in the wastebasket is made in 2.5 seconds.

Improves competitive position: color is an obvious built-in advantage when compared to ordinary black-and-white.

Grabs attention: any element stands out simply by being different from its black-and-white surrounings, creating curiosity and thus attracting attention to itself. Color identifies warranties, prices, offer expiration dates, payment information, etc.

Simplifies complex information: color coding reduces visual search time by up to 80%. Procedure guides, technical manuals are more effective. It brings order to chaos.

Initiates action: highlighting a problem engages the recipients' interest, triggers faster reaction. Problems are resolved faster, more efficiently.

Spotlights key elements: diagrams, charts and graphs are easier to understand when crucial components look different from their context.

Makes large documents less intimidating: visually breaking them into their component parts by color makes them smaller; making important information stand out makes it more accessible, more user-friendly and reader-friendly.

Highlights changes: color makes revisions stand out, helping the user to identify current information.

Organizes information: color used consistently throughout a document or series of documents becomes a classifying factor, cues the viewer to recognize elements for the kind of thing they are.

Increases impact of personal data: variable data specific to the recipient is flattering, irresistible. Ordinary documents become extraordinary and trigger results. 'Remaining balance' printed in color on an instalment-buying form raised payment-in-full from 20% to more than 50%.

Improves utility: data-based information is more useful if parts of that information specifically relevant to the user stand out in color. For instance: a price list with distributor's wholesale prices in red communicates more effectively.

* Statistics cited on this and the next page are quoting a variety of published studies

Color focuses observation: concentrates viewers' attention and makes them notice critical information. Medical, geological diagrams, wiring charts, circuit board layouts... any visually complex delineation.

Gives warnings: color makes safety precautions visible and alerts the viewer to danger to life or property. Red means stop. Yellow means caution.

Increases participation: by isolating and thus making crucial information more visible, it increases readership and the reader's involvement and caring about the information. In a study of 25,000 magazines, ads had 52% higher readership when color was added.

Lengthens attention span: by using color to emphasise what the writer/editor deems important, the reader is held by up to 82% longer.

Speeds learning: it makes the important matter stand out from the background, prompting the processing of information by classified hierarchy. Presentations are 70% clearer when color focuses on important details.

Improves recall : memory is triggered by visual stimuli, placement,and relationships to surroundings. Color increases recall by up to 60% in educational materials and training manuals if it is used functionally to organize the pages. Students remembered 25% more when their texts were highlighted in red.

Helps recognition: brand identification increased 70% when color was added.

Reduces errors: color focuses peoples' attention, thus helps them to fill out questionnaires and forms 50% more accurately.

Expands motivation: by displaying the "what's in it for me value" to the viewer, color generates excitement and enthusiasm. One study showed a 26% improvement in tendency to act.

Sells more: color attracts more readers than the equivalent black-and-white page. It induces them to pay attention, react—and buy (up to 85% more). Ads in the Yellow Pages get 44% more response when red is used.

Persuades: favorable response to the printed page creates favorable reactions to the ideas and influences favorable decisions. Color can show a concept or a new product in its best light. Proposals become more acceptable.

Boosts productivity: when used effectively color adds value through improved readability, more obvious clarity, fewer errors, longer recall, more accurate comprehesion, faster reaction.

Using color in business documents is a rational skill. It is not an artistic, subjective or personal form of self-expression. Using color in this working world has little to do with instinct or "liking," and everything with deliberate effectiveness. The goal is to blend the meaning of the message with astute visual techniques that help to explain the message and so to catapult it off the page into the individual reader's mind.

But what about Creativity? Unfortunately, this much overused word comes up whenever "design" is talked about. Too often it is misunderstood to mean inventing the weird, the new, the unexpected, as though being different were in itself a virtue. It is not. Being clear is far more valuable.

Having ideas is wonderful, of course. The question is whether they are good or bad, useful or misleading. The worst ideas are usually the ones that are stolen from somewhere else and grafted onto your product, whether they make substantive sense or not. The best ideas grow organically out of the material itself, responding to the document's needs and purposes. To create a standard of credibility, dependability, and trustworthiness, concentrate on:

Empathy: Think like your reader. Speak to a specific audience. Satisfy its needs.

Relevance: Make the presentation fit the document's purpose. Don't decorate.

Courage: Catch attention with images unexpected in the document's context.

Humor: Humanize your subject with visual and editorial punning.

Imagination: Combine elements in inventive ways to achieve intellectual sparkle.

Teamwork: Pool the talents and knowledge of all involved in the document.

Discipline: Insist on fine crafstmanship, precision, consistency to create excellence.

How do people use a document? Every reader is first a looker, quickly scanning the pages to find that nugget of information that is valuable to that individual. The looker becomes a reader when the writer persuades him or her that there is something in there worth while bothering with.

That is why you must make publications friendlier, easier to enter, easier to understand, faster to find things in. They must have a "first-glance value" that will make them essential immediately. They must display the "what's-it-about" and "what's-in-it-for-me" factors. That is why the message must be planned, constructed and written in such a way that color can be used to identify the valuable nuggets in it. Nuggets are special. Color should be earmarked to reinforce their specialness.

How can color help? Everything in print must be perceived by the user as giving better service, more concisely, faster. Color can highlight that service. It can be used to focus on explicit data. That is why color must be seen as a functional material, not just as a decorative one. It has to be used to add intellectual value, not just to catch attention. It must be used to enlighten, not merely to dazzle. It is vain to hope that a pretty-looking page will sell the information it contains. It will be swamped in our visually competitive environment. To fulfill its purpose, color must be functional as well as pretty. It must be used to reinforce the message.

Used functionally, color is much more than a cosmetic added to the surface of an existing page. "Colorizing" a bit here or a bit there just because color is available, without simultaneously using it for worthwhile emphasis, is mere prettification and a waste. Color has to be used as an integral part of a coordinated effort to make the information in print faster and easier to understand. It should only be used to *highlight the rarest and brightest elements.* It is a reinforcement of signals.

As such, it is a partner with typography, page architecture, infographics, and most of all—the writing and editing process. Its visual characteristics must be exploited **to help turn information chaos into organized and enthusiastic understanding.**

2 Ten commandments on using color

Thou shalt combine visual appeal with meaning

Color is appealing. In our information-overloaded society, the more appealing the message, the more likely is it to capture the attention of its audience. But prettiness is not enough. Color must also mean something.

Thou shalt assign color deliberately to fulfill specific functions

Color is not exciting by itself—it is everywhere. Only when it is coupled with intellectual meaning can it achieve valued significance.

Thou shalt use color to guide viewers to fast comprehension

Color is different from black. That is what makes it special in print. Use it sparingly, with discrimination.

Thou shalt avoid weakening color's power by overuse

Color is noticed only if it is bright enough, large enough, conspicuous enough, rare enough.

Thou shalt not use color just because it is available

Never use color just to dress up the publication. Use it only if the message is the better for it. It must be more than embellishment.

Thou shalt use color to explain, not to decorate

Don't be content with making the publication "pleasing to the eye." Use color to lead the eye to worthy material.

Thou shalt use color to sharpen the delivery of your message

Decide where the greatest value for the reader lies, then use color to make it stand out. Color must work for its living: it must add value.

Thou shalt establish character by consistent color use

Predictability creates comfort, recognition, personality. Build identity with disciplined color, type, spacing and page architecture.

Thou shalt use color to provide continuity

Most publications are part of a series. "Belonging" is advantageous both to the item and its publisher. Each issue is your representative.

Thou shalt plan for color use from the start of the project

Colorizing by retrofitting cannot do justice to color's capacity as a functional, rational, intellectual material. Plan for its purposeful utilization.

Notice the color of the panel's background: it is the palest screen of red. It defines the area, and makes the Commandments stand out as a group, special and different from the rest of the publication. Yet it is not so strong as to be disturbing. It has been assigned a job to do and it does it quietly. A good example of functional use of color.

3 Where to use color

Documents represent work. They are expected to be dull, because they have usually been uninviting, ordinary. Color can make them extraordinary. It can change that negative perception by giving the recipient a reason to enter, because it looks like cheerful, friendly material. But it is more than just that: since people look at the brightest and "different" area first, color can be used to prioritize information in a document. It can be used to organize the content, explain the structure, highlight the benefits. The more important an item is, the more colorful and noticeable it should be.

Write the text in such a way that it will benefit from color. Plan the writing to allow key factors to be visually emphasized. When the visual form works with the verbal content, the result is irresistible.

Accent whatever is of greatest self-interest to the recipient. The "What's in it for me" factor in a document is the bait on the hook that will pull the potential reader into reading. Your special offer... the phone number where help can be reached... the expiration date of their policy... a warning about their safety... whatever concerns them most.

Emphasize the main points in the text. Make the particularly cogent paragraph stand out by running it in color. Lead the eye to the positive results of a series of actions, highlight the benefits, the advantages. Pinpoint the topic under discussion (but not the headings; they already stand out in type, so it is probably a waste of effort to use color on them as well—unless there is another good reason to do it).

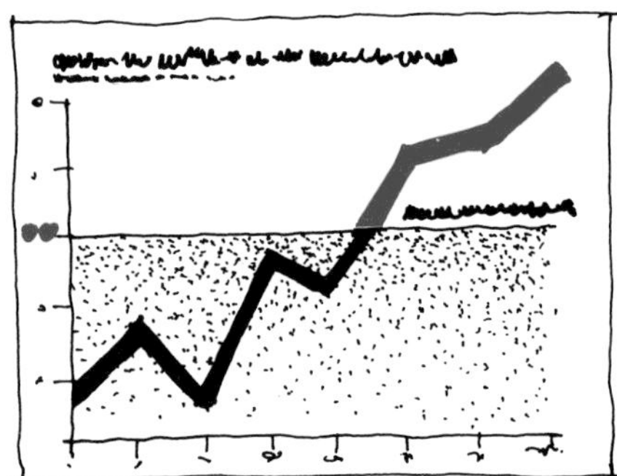

Pinpoint the main feature in text or graphics. Focus the viewer's attention to whatever you want them to notice: data that exceed the norm... profit or loss on the bottom line...

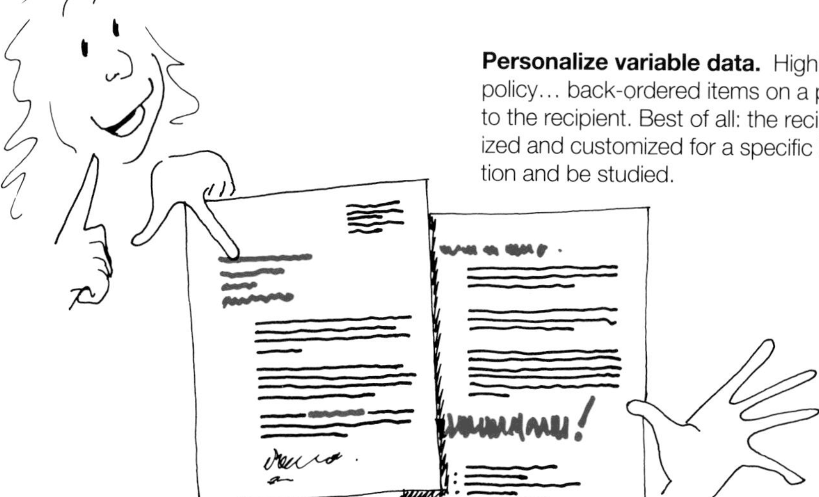

Personalize variable data. Highlight the specifics of an insurance policy... back-ordered items on a parts list... anything that is particular to the recipient. Best of all: the recipient's name. Documents personalized and customized for a specific individual are most likely to get attention and be studied.

Alert the viewer to unexpected data. Bank overdrafts... exceeding the extension granted by the tax collector... values that exceed specific tolerances...

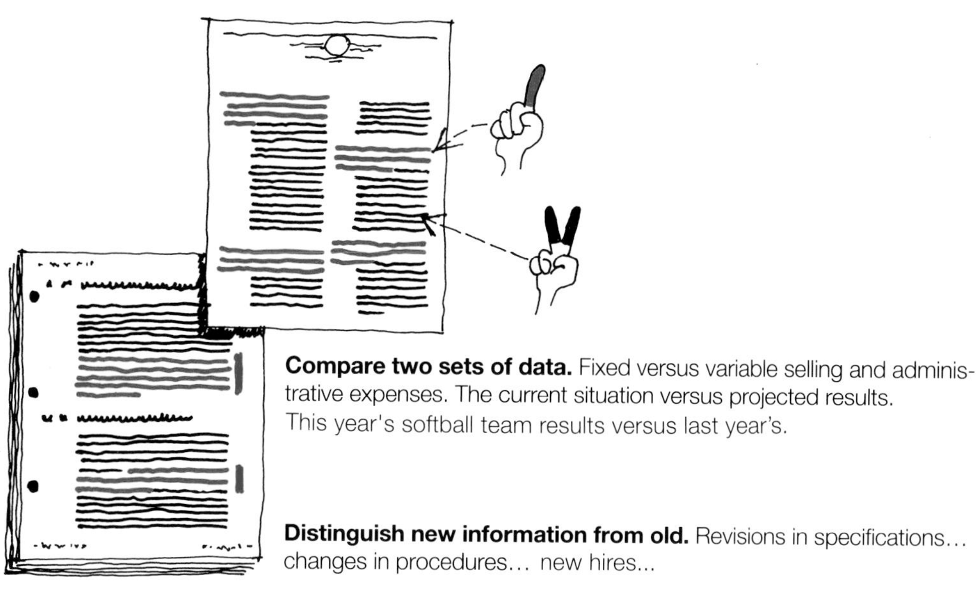

Compare two sets of data. Fixed versus variable selling and administrative expenses. The current situation versus projected results. This year's softball team results versus last year's.

Distinguish new information from old. Revisions in specifications... changes in procedures... new hires...

Classify rankings of numbers in a table. Identify shortfalls in red. Or, more elaborately: numbers exceeding a certain level are green, those at mid-level blue, below that in red. That uses the code of color meanings: green for good, go; red for danger, stop; blue for steadiness, credibility. Even if the table's construction is normal, color triggers recognition of the rankings, and desired interpretation at first glance.

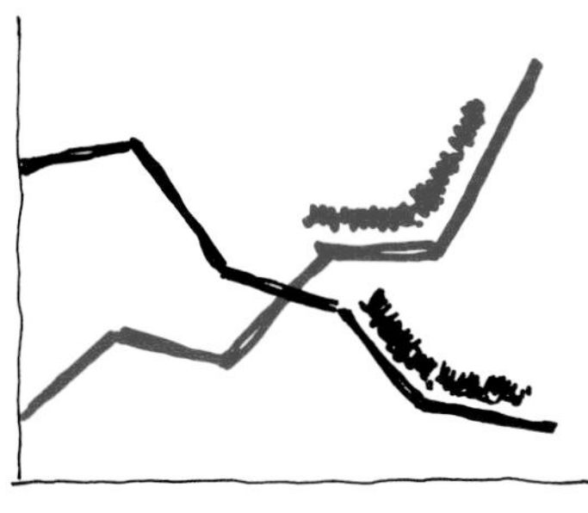

Link related elements with each other. Color intuitively bridges the gap between units on the page: the graph line in green and the green words that describe it... the red title and the red key paragraph of the text... the blue name with the blue quotation... the orange cause and its orange effect. Be aware of the linking capacity and never use it unintentionally because it misleads the viewer.

Separate the message from ancillary matter on the page. Identify page numbers, headers, footers, identifications, commands, logos, menu choices etc with color. By making these minor elements smaller, lighter, paler, less significant than the message, color is not used to attract attention, but merely to classify. That simplifies what the viewer sees, and makes technical documents less threatening.

Categorize areas of the page with color tints or boxes. Separate subsidiary information, background information, parallel information, footnotes, sidebars etc from the main body of the text. Use boxes only if the information needs to be broken into separate elements, and placing those elements in separate areas will help to explain it.

Make articles look shorter. Use color to distinguish various categories of information from each other. It helps the user to separate the background text from some of the other word-elements on the page: instructions… summaries… change revisions… biographies…locations… results… abstracts… conclusions …anything normally "boxed."

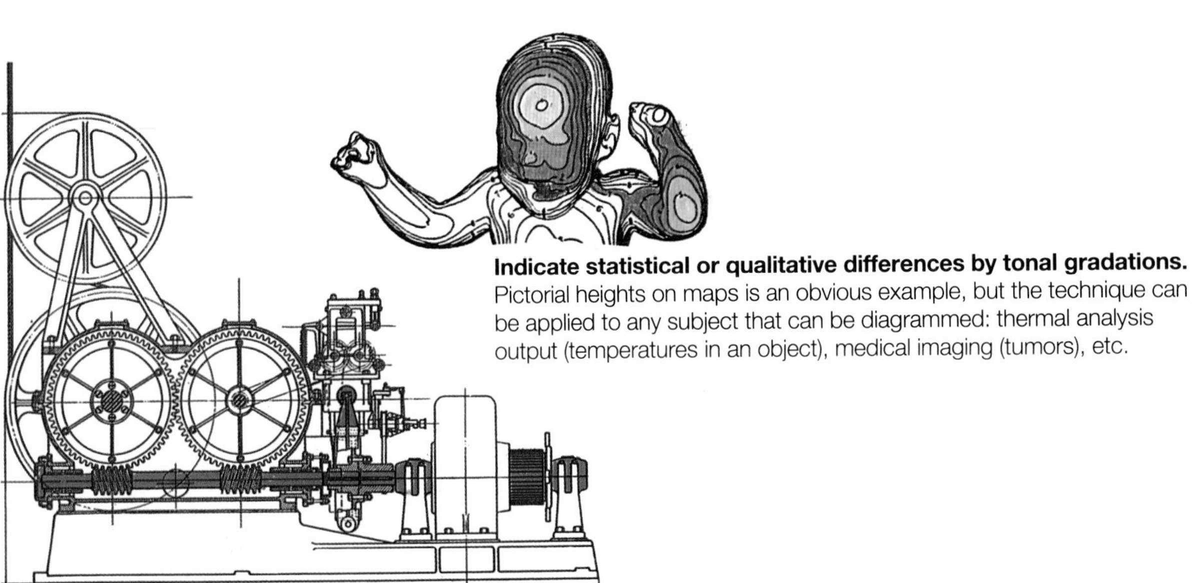

Indicate statistical or qualitative differences by tonal gradations. Pictorial heights on maps is an obvious example, but the technique can be applied to any subject that can be diagrammed: thermal analysis output (temperatures in an object), medical imaging (tumors), etc.

Simplify intricate technicalities. Codify components by assigned colors. Identify segments of a machine. On architectural plans separate plumbing from wiring, structure from air conditioning.

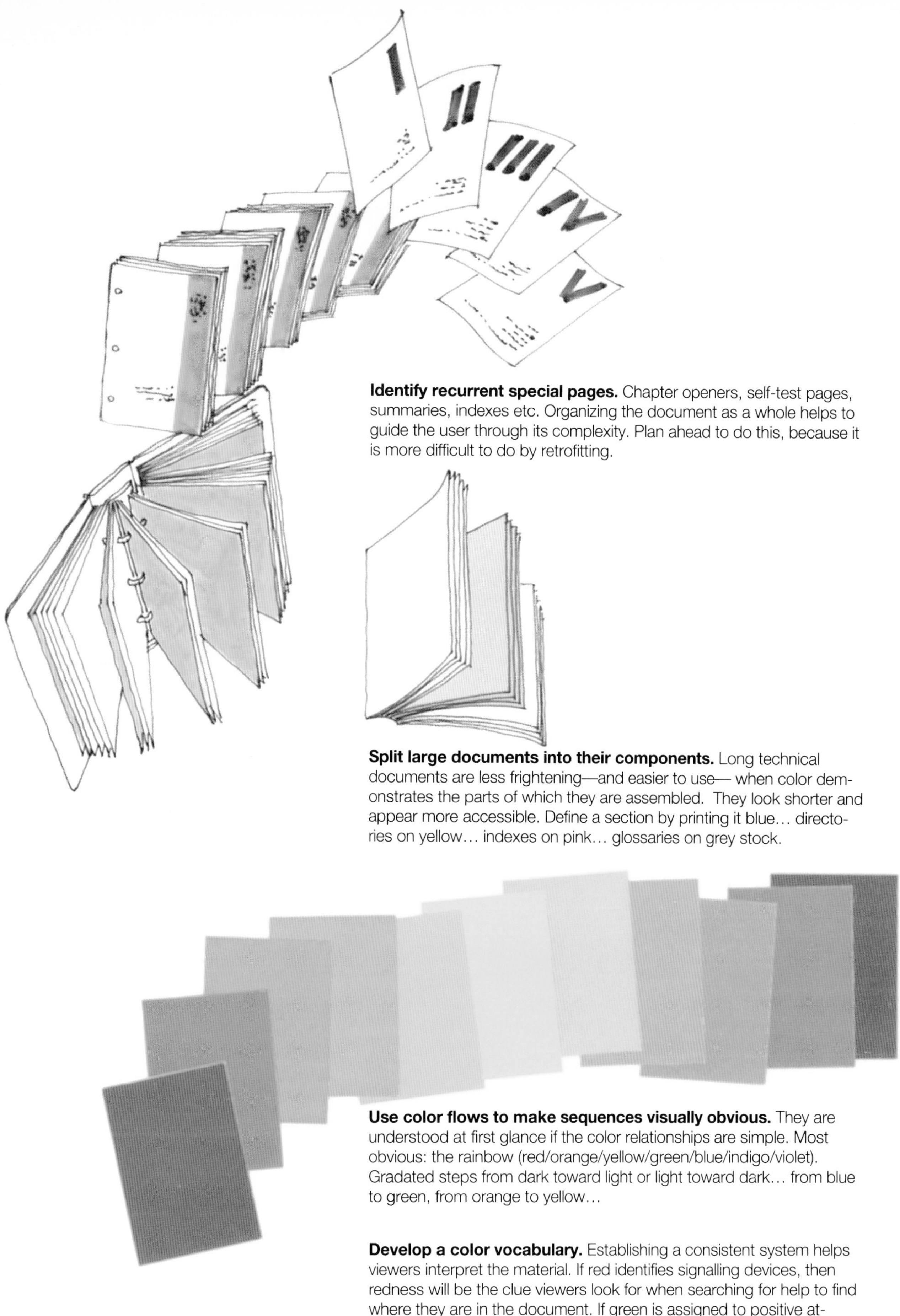

Identify recurrent special pages. Chapter openers, self-test pages, summaries, indexes etc. Organizing the document as a whole helps to guide the user through its complexity. Plan ahead to do this, because it is more difficult to do by retrofitting.

Split large documents into their components. Long technical documents are less frightening—and easier to use— when color demonstrates the parts of which they are assembled. They look shorter and appear more accessible. Define a section by printing it blue… directories on yellow… indexes on pink… glossaries on grey stock.

Use color flows to make sequences visually obvious. They are understood at first glance if the color relationships are simple. Most obvious: the rainbow (red/orange/yellow/green/blue/indigo/violet). Gradated steps from dark toward light or light toward dark… from blue to green, from orange to yellow…

Develop a color vocabulary. Establishing a consistent system helps viewers interpret the material. If red identifies signalling devices, then redness will be the clue viewers look for when searching for help to find where they are in the document. If green is assigned to positive attributes, then every time green appears in the document, the viewer will interpret the item as "good news." If menu choices are in blue and commands are in orange, arbitrarily switching them creates chaos.

4 How much color to use

Color is an immensely subtle artistic medium. Using it for a functional purpose in publications needs less subtlety. It demands simplicity, because its effectiveness depends on memory. Practical experience shows that people remember and recognize colors only in the broadest sense: redness, blueness, greenness, and the other basic hues for which there are specific names (yellow, grey, brown, pink etc).

Little spots are hardly noticeable and seldom worth the effort. Use color powerfully, with strength and boldness.

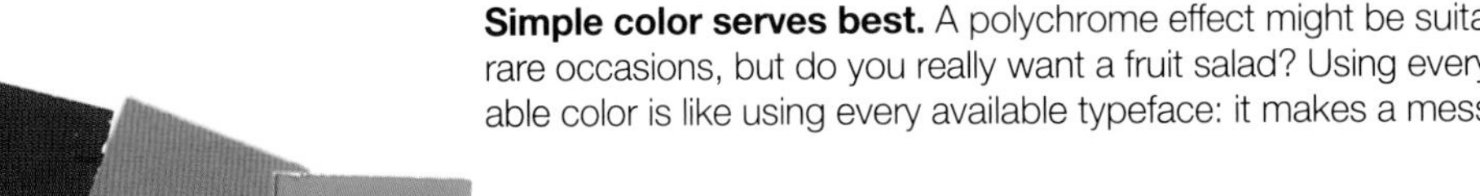

Simple color serves best. A polychrome effect might be suitable on rare occasions, but do you really want a fruit salad? Using every available color is like using every available typeface: it makes a mess.

Two colors in addition to black are understood and remembered best. The more colors there are, the more difficult it is to remember the meaning that each carries. Keep the code simple.

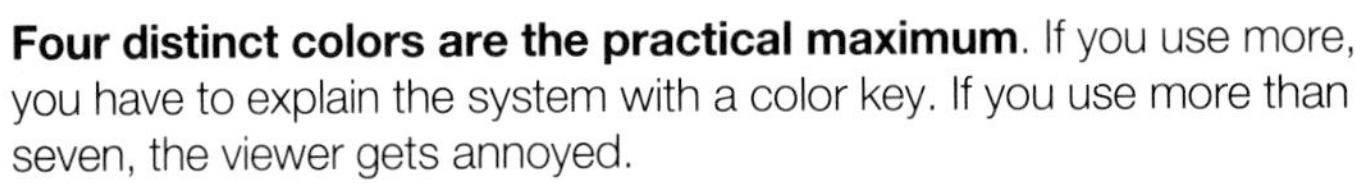

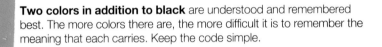

Four distinct colors are the practical maximum. If you use more, you have to explain the system with a color key. If you use more than seven, the viewer gets annoyed.

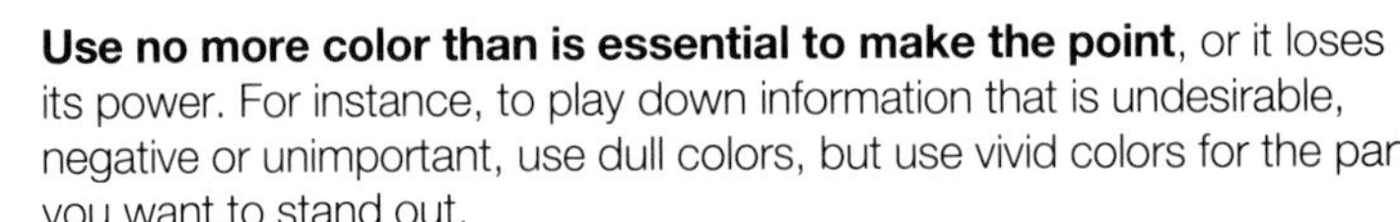

Use no more color than is essential to make the point, or it loses its power. For instance, to play down information that is undesirable, negative or unimportant, use dull colors, but use vivid colors for the part you want to stand out.

Use the same color coding throughout the entire range of publications and throughout the life of the project.

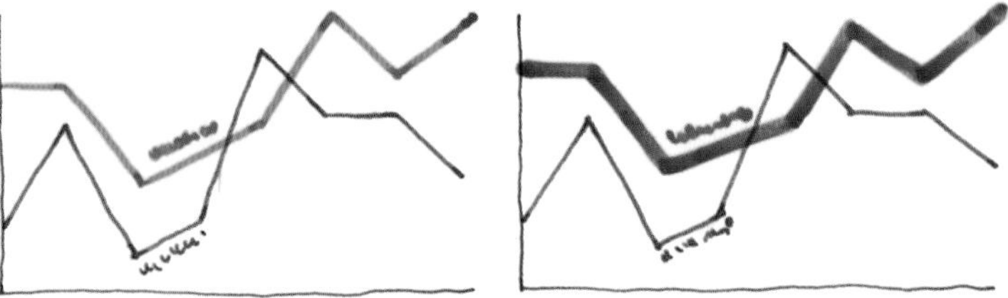

Duplicate color with shape. That is not redundant, but helpful. The emphasized line on a graph should not only be red, but fatter, so it

- attracts the eye more effectively
- is more striking and therefore more memorable
- helps people with impaired color vision
- is more discernible in bad light

Copying color in black and white

Since your pages are likely to be copied in black-and-white, do not rely completely on color to make diagrams intelligible (specially bar charts). Even if the black-and-white copier is highly sensitive to gray scale and well calibrated, it is likely that some of the colors will not look different

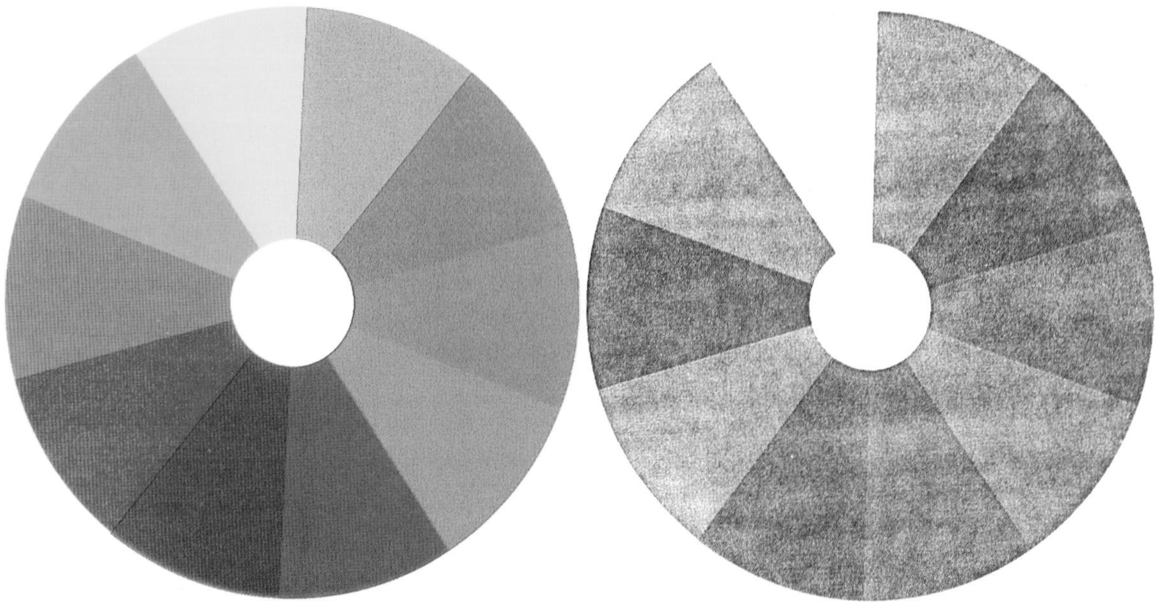

enough from each other. Others may surprise you. Therefore, clone the color differences with a variety of textures or hatch patterns. This is very important if the document is also shown as overheads in presentations and units are handed out in hard copy format.

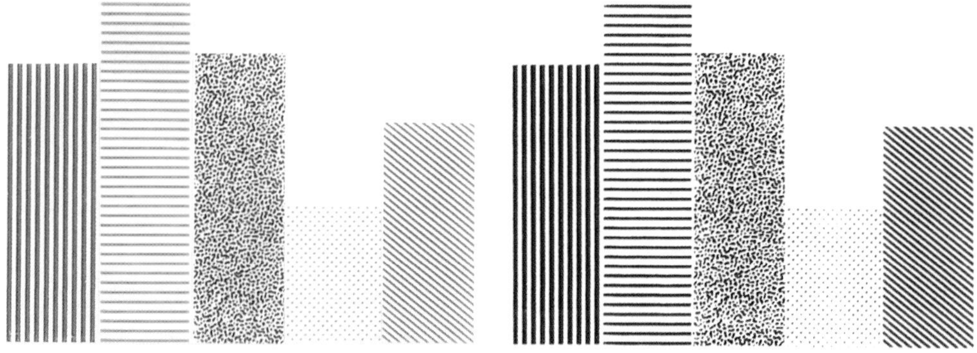

Use redundancy of both shape and texture to reinforce the color differences between areas.

Dark colors in the red range pick up best in black-and-white.

Pale blue and yellows do not pick up welll even in the best of copiers. Avoid them, if the likelihood of black-and-white copying is great.

Ensure strong contrast of tone between type and its background, so the type stands out legibly in the copy.

6 *Making the most of color*

Black is the most useful and flexible of all colors on the printed page. It is indeed a "color" on its own. Use the full range of effects that can be produced by screening:

To make a dark color appear paler, add paper. Paper? Right! The paper the toner is printed on reflects light. More paper shining through the toner creates the illusion of lightening the color. Since the toner is opaque, the only way to get more paper to shine through it is to break up the solid toner into a dot-like pattern with space between the dots: a

"screen." The smaller the dots and the bigger the space between them, the paler the effect. The color of the individual dots is always the same, solid hue of the toner, but their effect varies with their size and spacing. 100% coverage means that the toner is laid without a screen. 10% screen means that the dots are tiny, there is a lot of paper between them, and the result is very pale. Do not get confused with dpi or dots per inch, which is a measure of resolution, or fineness of the printer. The various percentages of the screens can be produced at any resolution. Also, do not be confused by the nomenclature of the "screens," "tints" and "tones" the manufacturer of your equipment may have chosen. Always go by their samples, choosing what looks right and specifying it the way they do.

Don't use just one screen. You can make it much richer and more interesting by adding a screen of black on top of the screen of color.

Beware of the brightness of colors. Just because some look brighter than others in the color sample book does not mean that they will be as powerful on the page as you hope. A sample may look strong when seen as a swatch, but when it is used for printing type, the result is disappointingly pale.That is because there are so many white spaces between the strokes of each letter, that it actually acts as though it were a screen of the color.

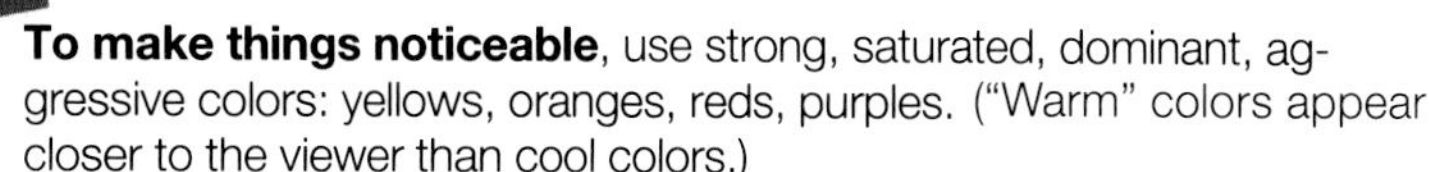

To make things noticeable, use strong, saturated, dominant, aggressive colors: yellows, oranges, reds, purples. ("Warm" colors appear closer to the viewer than cool colors.)

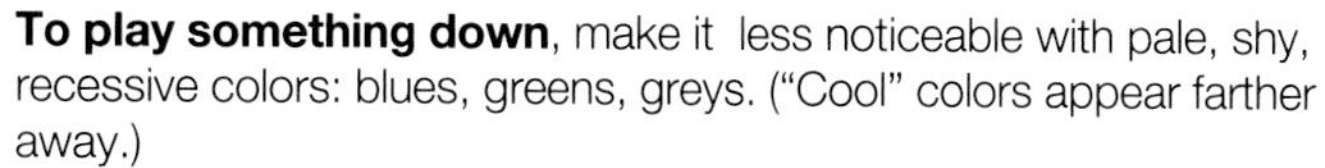

To play something down, make it less noticeable with pale, shy, recessive colors: blues, greens, greys. ("Cool" colors appear farther away.)

To identify important elements, use the warm, bright, active colors to ensure their being noticed first. Use the shy colors for contrast.

To make an area look smaller, color it dark in a quiet color.

To make a small area look larger, use any pale color.

Colors change with their background. No color exists by itself. Its neighbors affect it. Avoid disappointment: the color you pick will never be alone, so think ahead to its surroundings. Consider the relationships of colors to each other, rather than thinking only of individual colors. There are no new colors, so you canot be creative that way. There are only new color combinations which you manipulate. To make things more complicated: *The effect of a color changes as its proportion with its surroundings changes.* Alas, there are no simple laws or rules to follow. Try it out, look at it, then fix it.

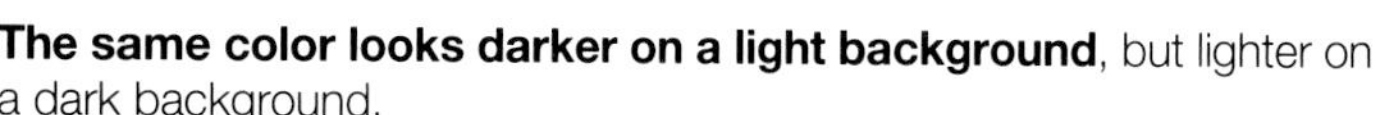

The same color looks darker on a light background, but lighter on a dark background.

The same color looks warmer on a cool background, but cooler on a warm background.

The same color looks different on a rough textured surface than on a smooth, shiny surface. Run a test to make sure of the result.

The same color looks different on colored paper. The only predictable fact: the result will be different from what you expect and the color will not appear to match the original. Test it out.

The same color looks different under different light. Ambient light affects a publication's perceived friendliness. In a dark office, bright colors and bigger type will be more effective, whereas in bright sunlight, subtler colors and smaller type are appropriate.

To identify related elements, use related colors. It is usually better to create peaceful harmony than clashing variety—even if such gaudiness appears cheerful and "colorful" at first glance. Play it safe and choose colors that are related in at least one, preferably two ways by:

- hue (the kind of color it is, e.g. its redness)
- saturation (the color's intensity, brightness, or "chroma")
- value (the color's shade, darkness/lightness).

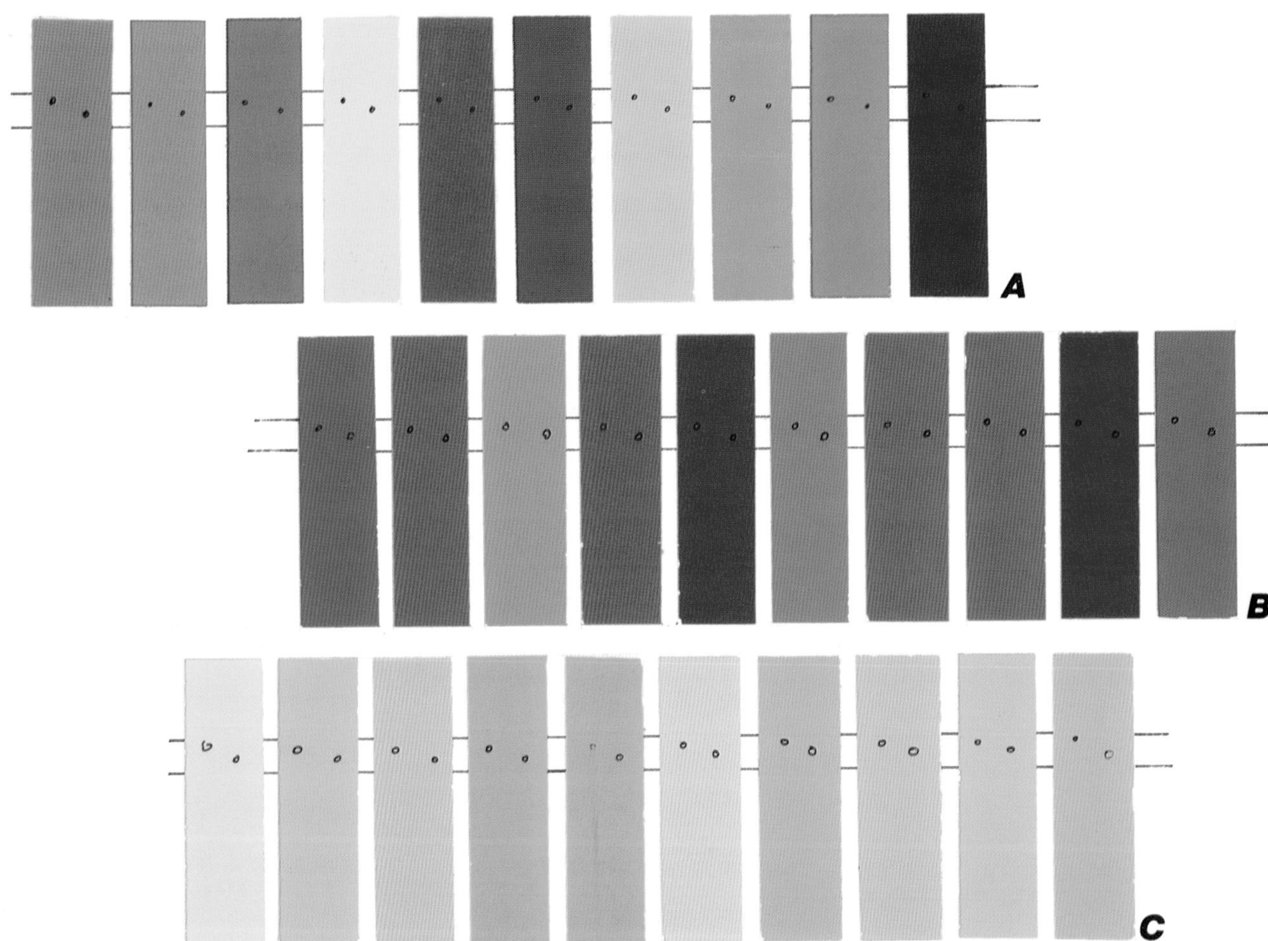

If each picket of a fence is painted in a color unrelated to its neighbors, some stand out, others recede. The fence looks colorful but irregular and gap-toothed **(A)**.

If the fence is painted in a variety of purples, the individual pickets can be picked out, yet the fence remains whole **(B)**.

If the pickets are painted in a variety of colors all of which share a similar tonal value, the pickets can be distinguished from each other, but the fence remains whole **(C).**

How does this affect your next bar chart?

Use color with your eyes open. Instead of blindly assuming that things will look like you want them or imagine them to be, realize that color can play tricks on you. Just be aware of what you are actually looking at.

7 Which color to choose

Do not pick a color just because you like it. Choose the color that will help the viewer interpret the message. The information's own logic should suggest how to handle it and which color to do it with.

Choose colors for their "value" and "chroma" rather than "hue." The hue (a color's blueness, redness, purpleness) is useful as a recognition factor to categorize information. Value (a color's darkness or lightness) makes it stand out against the paper. Chroma (a color's brigtness, saturation) gives brilliance or dullness. Value and chroma affect your communication goal more powerfully than the hue does.

Here and on the following pages, are a few generalizations about color. Some are derived from scientific surveys, others from observation. People using color seem to want these rules to raise their confidence in their own judgment. Unfortunately, there are no authoritative guidelines. There is only rational, analytical, practical good sense.

Choose the background color first. The temptation is first to pick the color highlighting the important parts and then conform the background to it. For a better result, decide on the large area (the background) first, and then conform the contrasting accents to it.

Use your common sense about the symbolism of color. In publications, the psychology of color matters less than where you use the color, how you use the color in relation to the meaning of the information, how much of it you use, and its noticeability (i.e.darkness/lightness contrast.)

About color preferences

Men prefer blue to red and darker, cooler colors...
but in reds they prefer yellowish ones.

Women prefer red to blue and warmer, lighter colors...
but in reds they prefer bluish ones.

Adults rank colors by preference thus:
blue...red...green...white...pink...purple...orange...yellow.

Children rank colors by preference thus:
yellow...white...pink...red...orange...blue...green...purple.

Color-preference:

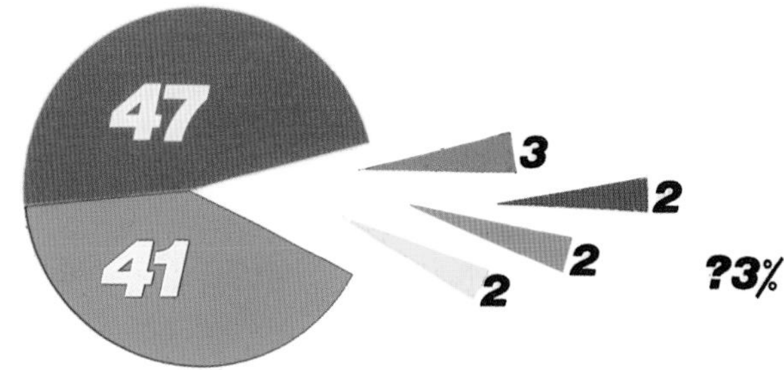

Read this only if you are curious. It could be interesting in terms of general knowledge. For practical purposes—skip it.

About the symbolism of color

Colors have psychological associations most of which are learned and vary among national, social and cultural groups. There are therefore no universally applicable rules. What appears exciting to some is merely vulgar to others. What is cheerful to some is depressing to others. Older people are made to feel distinctly uncomfortable by the clashing colors used by today's youth (which is perhaps why they use them). Lower income groups tend to prefer colors that are brighter than those chosen by upper income groups. If the color can be described in two words, "sky blue" "lemon yellow", then it is a lower-income color, whereas "greyish blue-green" needs three words and will be preferred by the more sophisticated higher-income people. But fashions change at an ever-faster rate, so even such a broad generalization only holds true temporarily. That is why advertisers and especially packagers invest fortunes in studying the trends of color preferences for their segment of the target market.

In the marketing sense, colors do indeed communicate subliminally and the recipients either "like" or "don't like" what they see. Much consumer acceptance depends on the first impression the object's color makes. In one famous experiment, tasters complained that coffee from a yellow can was too weak, from a dark brown can too strong, that from a blue can mild but with good aroma, and that from a red can just right. Of course, it was all the same coffee. A red car is thought to be faster than a car of any other color—and insurance premiums for red cars are higher, but that may be because young people buy them and they are the fast drivers.

In the supermarket, whiteness bespeaks purity (though whiteness is produced by chlorine, an environmentally unfriendly material, so in the future, purity is likely to be symbolized by unprocessed, unbleached earth colors.) Earth colors already symbolize natural products using no artificial preservatives. Pale colors suggest low calories. Blue is associated with club soda, skim milk, cottage cheese. Red is linked with heat, so it is never used on ice cream packages. Yellow stands for richness in butter and margarine. Silver and gold are expensive. Dark, vibrant and contrasting colors make a product like laundry powder strong.

Colors are used to idealize the character of the product: green peas are made greener with additives to make them more desirable. Colors also echo nature: bees and yellow-jackets are black and yellow: They sting. Ouch! Beware! That is why rat poisons are packaged in yellow-and-black... and many traffic signs are yellow-and-black. Yes, yellow and black is the most visible combination of colors. It is surely not a coincidence that both high visibility and danger are manifested the same way.

Red and yellow rooms feel warmer in terms of temperature, whereas blue rooms feel cooler. Experiments also show that blue schoolroomns are quieter and lead to better-behaved pupils who learn more. Darker rooms feel more constricting than paler ones. To make a small room feel bigger, paint it light.

Red is known to be exciting as a color, and green as more calming, but the effect is heightened or reversed by the degree of the color's paleness or darkness. Prison cells are now painted pale pink—it is apparently more relaxing than the pale green typical of institutions and hospitals. Red is also used in bars and casinos because it makes people less aware of the passage of time. This sounds far-fetched, but many of our stereotypes are founded on empirical experience and associations that have evolved over the years and become traditional. Red makes food more inviting (hence the maraschino cherry on top of the ice cream sundae) and by contrast, people eat less in blue rooms.

Pink boxes make the pastry they contain taste better. They also make cosmetics more valuable. On the other hand, orange shouts its presence, so it communicates accessibility, hence cheapness. It is informal, like the cheap hotels that use lots of orange (on the roof, in the plastic upholstery, carpets etc). Yellow is visible at greatest distances, so it is used for traffic signals, taxicabs, buses. It can also help to sell a house faster with yellow signs, daffodils in the front and in the vases inside. It is a cheerful color, but too much of it creates nervous tension, so babies cry more in yellow rooms.

Dark blue commands respect. It symbolizes authority, trustworthiness, seriousness. That is why bankers, lawyers, professors should wear it. Black is an even more authoritative color for mens' suits, and is ideal for the bank president, but not the junior clerk. Brown lacks the authority of blue or black, though it has friendliness and approachability. However, green is very rarely seen as a suit color (except in Austria where Loden green is a national symbol). Green is obviously an environmentally meaningful color. On the other hand, it is also the ideal color used as a separator between packages of meat at the supermarket meat counter, since it is the complementary color to red, and thus makes the meat appear fresher, juicier and more irresistible. Don't send green mailers to farmers in the summer. They are surrounded with the color, so your appeal won't stand out. Use red instead. But do use green in winter, when they will aniticipate its return and feel good about it.

Grey symbolizes creativity, success, and even elegance—except for people who live in bleak climates and who see it as dirty, grimy and depressing. White is clean, pure, and efficient. The nurse in white is deemed to be more competent than a nurse in any other color.

Does any of this matter in your context? Use your common sense.

Colors exist in relation to their surroundings. The proportions of one color to another change the effect. What you use color **for** is more important than the color you do it with.

About color associations

Elegant colors: Upmarket. High style. Expensive. Snob-value. Quality.

Gold, silver, copper, metallics, black, chocolate, grey, maroon, navy blue

Masculine colors: Anything used with restraint and minimally. The Royal Enclosure at Ascot.

Black, silver, grey, purple, port-wine red, old-leather brown, dark racing green.

Feminine colors: Gentle pastels. Misty. Sentimental. Caring. Loving. Springlike.

Pale blues, pale pinks, yellows, pale greys, flesh colors.

Fresh, clean, healthy colors: Cool water, dewy lawns, the scent of lime or lemon, outdoors.

Daffodil yellow, bright blue, bright greens of all kinds.

Natural colors: Security. Dependability. Food that grandmother used to make.

Browns, oranges, quiet greens, reds, golds, all earth colors.

Loud colors: Dominating. Vibrant. Aggressive. Shouting. Vivid.

Primary (red, yellow, blue) **secondary** (orange, green, purple) **colors. Black., white,**

Quiet colors: Peaceful. Passive. Unassuming. Dull.

All colors that are muted and subdued.

Clashing colors: Dynamic. Exciting. Startling. Don't overdo this!

Unexpected combination of any two or more colors.

Cool colors: Recessive. Calm. Sedating. Status. Remote. OK for large areas on the page.

Blue, green, pale yellow, pale pink , pale purple, violet.

Warm colors: Cheeful. Stimulating. Active. Fun. Requiring response. Only for small areas on the page.

Red, orange, yellow, purple.

Light colors: Soft. Transparent. Airy. Quiet. Shy. Fine for backgrounds.

Any hue with white in it.

Dark colors: Heavy. Dense. Depressing. Ponderous. Dignified. Expensive. Best for type.

Red, purple, green, blue, brown.

Your favorite color:

Does it fit your image?

The following words are not poetry, but an attempt at describing some of the psychological implications of basic colors in our culture.

About the psychological implications of color

Red hot... passionate... bloody... horrifying... burning...fire... sunset... revolutionary... dangerous... active... aggressive... vigorous... impulsive... crude... bankrupt... Stop!

Yellow energetic... bright... optimistic... cheerful... sunny... active...stimulating... noticeable... memorable... intellectual... cowardly... imaginative...idealistic... Caution!

Green natural... fertile... restful... calm... refreshing... financial... prosperous... growing... youthful... abundant... healthy... envious... diseased...decaying... Go!

Blue serene... calm... loyal... clear... cool... peaceful... tranquil...excellent... just... watery... hygienic... distant... conservative...deliberate... spiritual... relaxing... first prize

Dark blue romantic... moonlit... discouraging... stormy

Khaki military... drab... warlike

Pink fleshy... sensuous... cute... romantic... sweet... cloying

Orange warm... autumnal... gentle... informal... affordable... wise... cheap

Brown earthy... mature... ripe... obstinate... reliable... conscientious...stolid...parsimonious

Sepia old...faded

Purple royal... luxurious... churchly... pompous... valuable... highest award... powerful... ceremonial... vain... nostalgic... mourning... funereal

White cool... pure... true... innocent... clean... hygienic... trustworthy... simple... honest

Grey neutral... secure... stable... mature... successful... affluent... safe...retrospective... discreet... wintery... old... calm

Black authoritative... respectful... powerful... strong... present... practical... solemn... dark... morbid... despairing... evil... empty... heavy... frightening... dead

Gold sunny... majestic... rich... wise... honored... expensive

Silver high tech... moonlit

These expectations of reactions are only broad generalizations and they may or, may not be valid. Nationality, age, environment, experience, social and economic class, all affect how people react to different colors. Also, many groups of people have developed color symbolisms as a specialized vocabulary of their professions. Furthermore, the language of color differs by culture. In the Orient, for instance, colors can signify particular classes of trade and represent religious and traditional meanings. Be aware of them, if your publication is targeted at specific demographic groups. However, everything depends on the specific hue and its shade, brilliance, and proportion to its surroundings. So, in the words of the cynical philosopher: *all generalizations are false, including this one.*

8 Combining colors with colors

Do not choose *colors*. Plan *effects*. Base choice on hue (the color itself) in conjunction with value (the darkness of the color). They are separate properties and vary widely. Violet, for instance, is much darker than yellow, so its effect is very different from yellow's. Color for documents is chosen by logical analysis. It has nothing to do with what color you like, because it is nothing like painting your bedroom. The purpose of color is less about making good-looking pages and more about using it to explain, emphasize, organize, draw the eye, affect interpretation. You are looking for relationships, balance, contrast, proportion.

Harmony is what people normally seek. It is achieved by finding colors that "go well together." It guarantees a safe—and bland—result. However, it is not totally reliable, because what may be harmonious to some is distinctly less so to others.

Contrast creates noticeability. Black-on-white creates the maximum tonal contrast. Black-on-yellow is more noticeable. In fact, it is so aggressive that it hurts. That is why it is seen on traffic signs but seldom in bulk on the printed page. It works well as a small accent.

Pure chroma stands out. The purer the chroma (brilliance, brightness), the more visible it is at a distance and the more noticeable it is close up. The subtler the color's chroma (the more it comes to neutral grey), the more difficult it becomes to distinguish the color.

Reserve the brilliance of bright colors for special accents.

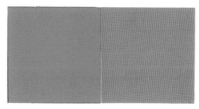

Use quieter colors for large areas. Do not make the brightest color also the largest area.

Full-strength colors in equal areas create garishness.

Using one color as the dominant and other colors as accents or support creates the most effective schemes in print.

Avoid red/green combinations, especially to distinguish factual elements. Most color-impaired people suffer from this deficiency.

Pick your color scheme from one of these:

1. **Corporate identity guidelines**. If you are lucky enough already to have some established palette, learn to understand it and use it with careful purpose.

2. **Similar documents** that you admire. Borrowing techniques is not plagiarism, nor is it something to be ashamed of. "Originality" and "creativity" are misunderstood and overused concepts, misplaced in the working world of functional communication. It's not what material you use but what you do with it that matters.

3. **Any of the guidebooks** on color schemes commercailly available at artist-supply stores and most bookshops.

4. **No-color** color scheme: just black, greys and white. Black is indeed a "color." Flatter it with a technical-sounding name: "*achromatic*."

5. **Black-plus-one-color.** The "highlight" scheme is the commonest in print. All colors go well with black. Bright colors go best with pale grey. Pale colors go best with dark grey.

6. **Schemes based on the color wheel**. The wheel organizes colors according to the spectrum. It is divided into ten segments. Locate one color and then use the following short-cuts to establish relationships:

Colors that lie directly across the wheel.
(Complementary scheme). To avoid garish effects, do not use full-strength colors in areas of the same size. Instead, use the quieter of the two for large areas, the brighter one as small accents.

Colors that are separated by one segment.
(Analogous scheme). Since they are so closely related, they tend to be harmonious, especially if one of them is clearly the dominant.

Colors that are separated by three segments.
(Contrasting scheme). They need not clash unpleasantly, if the duller is used for background and the brighter as accent.

Colors that are variations within a segment.
(Monochromatic scheme). Lighter and darker, or yellower and bluer versions of red, for instance. Realism and shading is normally achieved by using monochromatic color groups.

9 Color and panels

Difference in color separates an area from its surroundings. It marks it as a special element on the page. Inserting color panels is also an easy way to make the pages look richer and more interesting—as long as the color is not overwhelming. Charts, tables, graphs, illustrations, boxes, etc. are a good opportunity for such ernrichment.

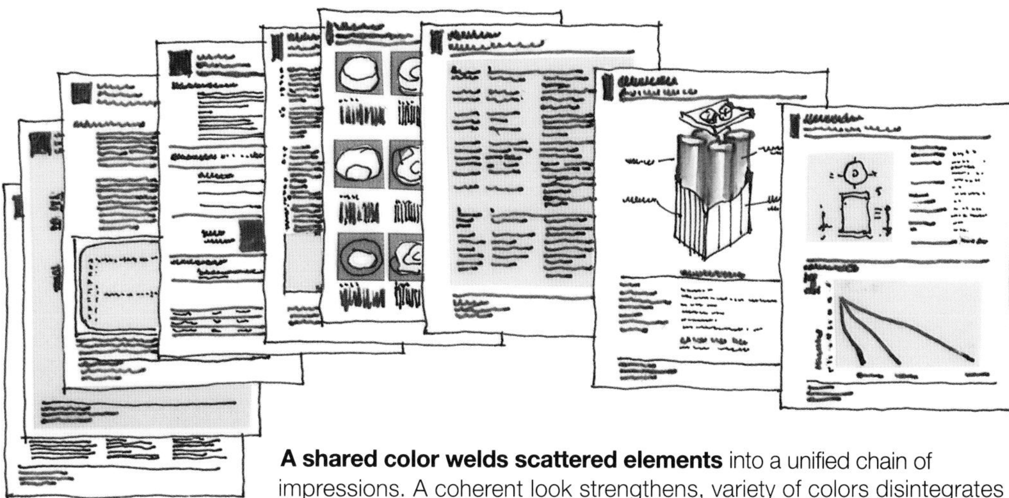

A shared color welds scattered elements into a unified chain of impressions. A coherent look strengthens, variety of colors disintegrates the publication. The most unified result is gained by using only one hue for backgrounds.

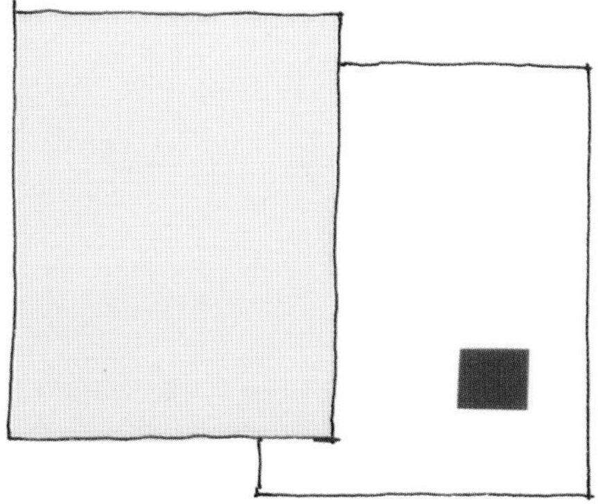

The larger the area, the lighter the color should be. The smaller the area, the more saturated the color can be. Large areas of color look more saturated than small ones that use the same color, no matter what color you use.

Use only the lightest colors as a background for type. Ease of legibility depends on high contrast between the type and the background on which it is seen. We are used to and expect the maximum contrast: black on white. Color background reduces the contrast. Take no risks, make it pale, never darker than a screen of

- 20% for the yellows and light blues.
- 15% for red and green.
- 10% for purple or brown.

m mmmm mmmmmmm mmmmmmm mmm mmmmmmm	m mmmm mmmmmmm mmmmmmm mmm mmmmmmm
mmmmmmm mmmmm mmm mmmmmm mmm	mmmmmmm mmmmm mmm mmmmmm mmm
mm mm mmmmmmm mm mmm mmmm mmmmm mmm	mm mm mmmmmmm mm mmm mmmm mmmmm mmm
mmmmm mm mmmmm mm m mm mmmm mmm	mmmmm mm mmmmm mm m mm mmmm mmm
mmmm m mmmm mm mmmm mm mmm mmmmm	mmmm m mmmm mm mmmm mm mmm mmmmm

Use bars of equal value of color for tables. Help the eye track from side to side by color strips, but avoid creating easier-to-read versus harder-to-read comparisons. Since black is easier to read on white than on a darker background, the wording in the black-on-white rows stands out more. Controlling the value solves the problem of inequality of importance.

Use gradient fills to create motion. Ramping or gradation is a technique in which screens change from dark to light in small steps, giving the illusion of smooth tonal change. The eye normally travels from the richer, darker side towards the lighter, paler side.

Print the most important information at the light end of the ramp for maximal contrast. That way you lead viewers to what you want noticed. They are bound to study it first, leaving the less contrasty area till later, mistaking it for unimportant, supporting background.

Place the important material on the dark side if you are using white lines or type on a colored background (i.e. the reverse of the previous scheme).

Watch out for moiré patterns when printing one screen on top of another to create mixed colors. The tiny marks combine with one another to make unwanted stars or lines. Check to make sure that the equipment is calibrated to the correct "angling" of the screens.

10 Color and pictures

Avoid printing black-and-white photos in color. They look pale and washed-out, because the contrast of color-to-white is weaker than that of black-to-white. Thus even the darkest areas can only be as dark as the darkness of the color you are using. The darker the color, the richer the result. Dark blue, dark green, are best. Red blushes pink.

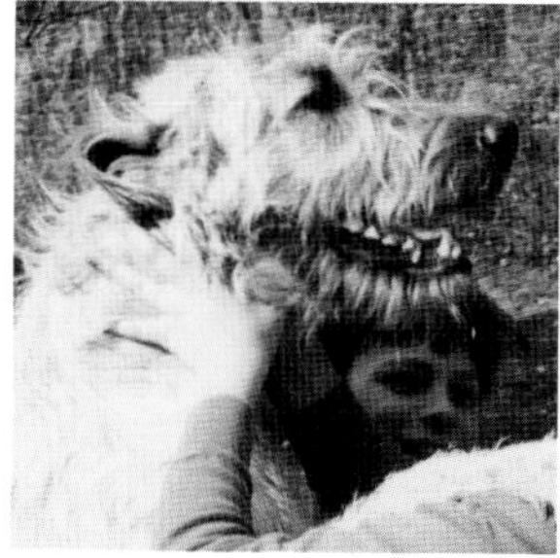
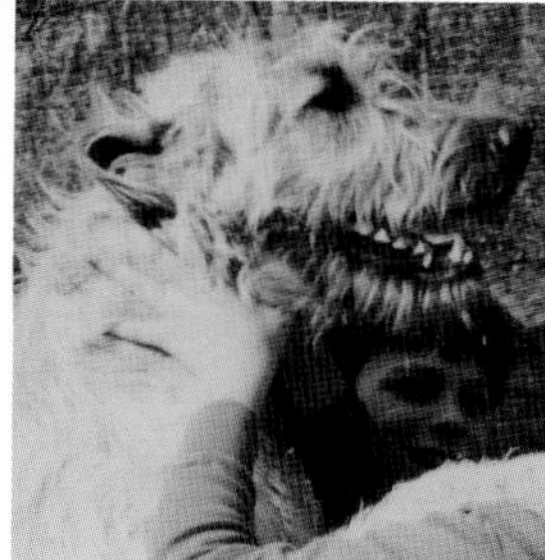

BLACK WITH 20%... 60%... 80% CYAN

Avoid printing a color screen over a black-and-white photo, even though it looks more colorful. The color blankets all areas alike, darkens the highlights, and robs the picture of its contrast and sparkle.
Do it only if colorfulness is more valuable to the *publication*, than the details in the photo would be to the *individual reader*.

BLACK HALFTONE WITH CYAN HALFTONE

For maximum impact, make duotones from black plus another color. A duplicate halftone is surprinted in color on top of the black halftone. Dark areas are reinforced, while light areas remain open, enhancing the intensity of the image, and giving it a touch of subtle hue.

BLACK/YELLOW... CYAN/YELLOW... CYAN/MAGENTA DUOTONES

Create unexpected results by running duotones in unexpected combinations of colors. Or change the balance of the components in normal duotones by strengthening one, or "shortening" the other. Experiment!

BLACK/MAGENTA...

Create startling effects by printing high-contrast duotones over a very light screen of a third, pale color. This is an area for courageous experimentation because variations are endless.

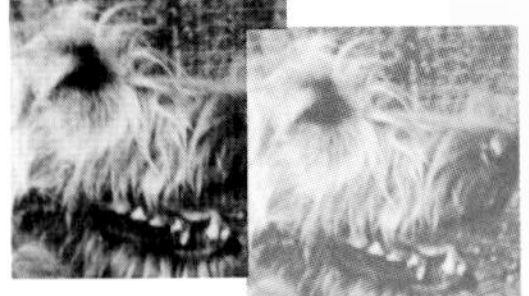

BLACK/MAGENTA ON 20% YELLOW SCREEN

Nothing replaces the credibility of full color. The world is colorful and four-color process represents it most realistically. Its four component colors (**C**yan, **M**agenta, **Y**ellow, and Blac**K**) are balanced to blend into the illusion of reality when printed on top of each other.

You can find walls painted in this daring shade of orange in Malmö, Sweden. Extending the wall's color into the panel below increases the drama and helps focus on the reason why the picture was published.

THE SHUTTERS NEED FRESH PAINT

Expand the impact of a full-color picture by matching one of its colors elsewhere on the page. If the subject of a box is related, the color will link them. If the headline is related, the color will link them.

Weaken panels by color. Panels dominate color pictures because they are visually so simple. A color different from the photo reinforces their contrast, but matching weakens it, bringing them into balance. Gentle ramps look much more natural when panels are near photos.

Too much spice spoils the soup. Unlimited special graphic effects are possible using various software capabilities: mezzotint textures, polarization, posterization, superimposition, etc. They can give sparkle and graphic dash to the page. Watch out. Less is more.

11 Color and type

Blacktype on white paper works best for text. That is why it is "normal." Printing it in color carries a risk: it goes against habit. If the material in color is remarkable enough, (and short enough), the reader will pay attention because it is "different," despite habit. But do not overdo it, or it will lose its surprise value.

Black type on white paper has the best contrast for legibility. Printing the same type in color reduces that contrast, because colors are paler than black. Color arouses curiosity, but reduces legibility. Some colors (e.g. yellow) are paler than others (e.g. violet). Weigh the loss of contrast against the advantage of colorfulness. Weigh the cost/benefit ratio. Every decision costs something.

The oppressor's wrong, the proud man's contumely,
The pangs of despised love, the law's delays,
The insolence of office, and the spurns
That patient merit of the unworthy takes,
When he himself might his quietus make
With a bare bodkin? Who would fardels bear,
To grunt and sweat under a weary life,
But that the dread of something after death,
The undiscover'd country from whose bourn
No traveller returns, puzzles the will,
And makes us rather bear those ills we have
Than fly to others that we know not of?
Thus conscience does make cowards of us all;
And thus the native hue of resolution
Is sicklied o'er with the pale cast of thought,

The oppressor's wrong, the proud man's contumely,
The pangs of despised love, the law's delays,
The insolence of office, and the spurns
That patient merit of the unworthy takes,
When he himself might his quietus make
With a bare bodkin? **Who would fardels bear,
To grunt and sweat under a weary life,
But that the dread of something after death,
The undiscover'd country from whose bourn
No traveller returns, puzzles the will,
And makes us rather bear those ills we have
Than fly to others that we know not of?**
Thus conscience does make cowards of us all;
And thus the native hue of resolution
Is sicklied o'er with the pale cast of thought,

Compensate for color's paleness by using more of it. All printed colors are weaker than black To achieve impact equivalent to black's:

- make the element bigger (e.g. a size larger type)
- make the lines fatter (e.g. a bolder weight of type)
- make them both bigger and fatter

(That is why color should be reserved for page components and information important enough to warrant such emphasis.)

In all sorts of publications, you will find headlines or titles picked out in color, just because color is available and it makes the page look more attractive. Is there anything wrong with that? No. Its wide use proves that it is a perfectly acceptable technique.

As always, the context in which color is used affects the wisdom of using it. Where headings are expected to be run in black (as in regular newspapers, for instance), using a color is startling. If the title so uniquely treated is worthy of the distinction, the fact that it is startling and thus stands out against the others is not merely justified but an advantage. If, however, the title has been picked out in color arbitrarily, just to add a touch a "variety" and to "dress up the page," then its distinction is leading the public to a false interpretation. It has been made to appear more important than it deserves to be. The disappointed reader feels cheated, and the publication loses credibility.

The darker the color, the less difficult it is to read. A color may look strong in a sample, but looks pale and washed-out when used for type. That is because the text acts just like a "screen" letting a lot of white paper be seen between the strokes of the letters, where the color is. Pick a much darker color than you think you need.

Which is more important: what the article says, or the way you make it look cute? Surface prettiness can never substitute for substance. The look of the page may lure potential readers to pay attention at first glance, but the information they need lies in the body of the text. Don't let the flamboyance of the surface gloss become an obstacle to understanding. Don't make them notice the color and ignore the story. That's why you should pick only light tints for backgrounds to type.

What works and does not work. Here are some generally accepted principles which may or may not be true. Take them for what they are.

Best legibility for text	Black text on white (but not white text on black)
	Dark green text on white background
	Dark blue text on white background
	Brown text on white background
	Warm color text on cool colored background
Worst legibility for text	Red text on green
	Green text on red
	Blue text on yellow
	Green text on blue
	Red text on blue
	Black text on grey darker than 20%
	Black text on color that is darker than 20% black
	White text on black
	Any bright colored text longer than a paragraph
Best visibility to attract attention but not to use for text in bulk	Black on yellow
	Black on orange
	Orange on dark blue
	Green on white
	Red on white
	Dark blue on white
	White on dark blue
	Orange on black
	White on black
	White on green, red, or purple
	Purple on white
	Dark blue on yellow
	Dark blue on orange
	Yellow on black
	Yellow on dark blue
	Purple on yellow

For text type in color, do as many of the following as you can:

Increase the type size.
Use a bolder weight of type.
Make lines a little shorter than usual.
Add an extra sliver of space between the lines.
Avoid peculiar typefaces that are hard to read.
Choose a sans-serif face.
Avoid condensed or expanded or oblique type.
Avoid too many words set in capital letters.
Keep type normal (let color do the shouting).

Color should emphasize the important point

Color should emphasize the important point

Color should emphasize the important point

Color should emphasize the important point

Color should emphasize the important point

Run key words in a title in black instead of color. Normally we make special elements stand out in color, because we think color is special. But color does not stand out as well as we think it does, since it is paler than black. Better think the other way: print the surrounding words in color and use black for maximal attention.

Color should emphasize the important point

Make surrounding words grey, to help the key words stand out in color—if you insist on color for them. Screening tones the black down and improves the balance.

Never screen type smaller than 18pt. It disintegrates the strokes of the letters and makes them illegible.

To be, or not to be: that is the question:
Whether 'tis nobler in the mind to suffer
The slings and arrows of outrageous fortune
Or to take arms against a sea of troubles,
And by opposing, end them? To die: to slee
No more; and by a sleep to say we end
the heart-ache and the thousand natural sh
That flesh is heir to, 'tis a consummation
Devoutly to be wish'd. To die, to sleep;

Avoid reversing type in white on a colored background. It is 40% more difficult to read than colored type on a white background. A few large words are no problem, but a whole paragraph of text will be skipped. Reading should be so natural and so easy that it should never demand deciphering. The reader should not be conscious of the act of reading. The best type is invisible.

For white type on color, do as many of the following as you can:

Pick a dark color for good contrast .

Use a solid color, not a screen.

Pick type that has strokes of even thickness.

Use a bold version of serif faces.

Avoid extrabold faces whose h●les ("e") cl●g.

Avoid condensed, expanded, or oblique faces.

Enlarge the type by one, preferably two, sizes.

Add a sliver of extra space between the lines.

Keep lines short.

Set ragged-right for normal word-spacing.

This is a sample of type representing text in bulk or any type set smaller than 14 point. Its purpose is to demonstrate the subtle relationship of type printed in color on a colored background, and to show how both noticeability and legibility vary. Choose colors that help reading, unless you want to create shock.

This is a sample of type representing text in bulk or any type set smaller than 14 point. Its purpose is to demonstrate the subtle relationship of type printed in color on a colored background, and to show how both noticeability and legibility vary. Choose colors that help reading, unless you want to create shock.

Choose subtle, quiet colors rather than aggressive, bright ones for backgrounds to colored type. Colored type on a bright background tires the eye faster than if it were on white... type is to be read, not red.

Make a test whenever colored type will print on a colored background—whether the background color is printed on white, or it is the color of the paper stock itself. There are no rules and the effects are unpredictable.

This is a sample of type representing text in bulk or any type set smaller than 14 point. Its purpose is to demonstrate the subtle relationship of type printed in color on a colored background, and to show how both noticeability and legibility vary. Choose colors that help reading, unless you want to create shock.

This is a sample of type representing text in bulk or any type set smaller than 14 point. Its purpose is to demonstrate the subtle relationship of type printed in color on a colored background, and to show how both noticeability and legibility vary. Choose colors that help reading, unless you want to create shock.

Be sure that there is at least 30% difference in tone value between the color of the words and of their background. Anything less will make the words invisible, no matter how bright the color. Plan early, so you can run experiments and avoid difficulties.

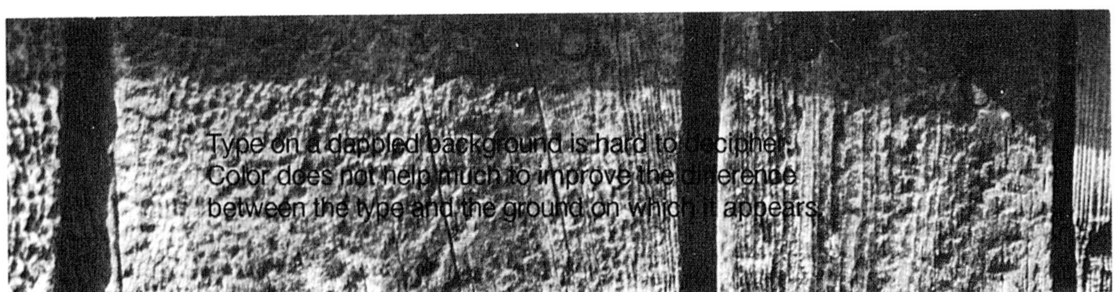

Type on a dappled background is hard to decipher.
Color does not help much to improve the difference
between the type and the ground on which it appears.

Avoid type on a picture, even if it is printed in color. It is harder to read if the background is mottled or textured. Color in the type or the picture (or both) does not help. It makes it worse.

Spark up non-typographic devices such as rules, bullets, bars etc. with color. However, be just as discriminating here as elsewhere in what to colorize. Color should reinforce a rational, calculated purpose. These elements are so easy to print in color that doing so has become hackneyed. If you do decide on the trick, then do it with gusto and bright colors. If you have to use a pale color, use bolder lines and bigger symbols.

Do not sacrifice legibility for graphic effect. The value of the document lies in its content, not in how loud it shouts.

12 How words, shape, space, and color produce impact

Example 1: **Blending form and content**

Write and design with color in mind

If you know before you start assembling your thoughts that color is going to be available, you can structure the organization of the writing to take advantage of the power that color can add to words in type. What you are about to read is an example. This version, written and displayed as running text, is the most common way of transmitting factual information. There's nothing wrong with it, but it does require concentrated study before the key points it contains are revealed. It is therefore slower than if it were written as a list, whose visible structure helps scanning. A list is a marriage of content with form, where the one cannot exist without the other. The very fact of its being seen as a list makes the information more inviting, because we know from experience that it will be quick and easy to take in. The visual tabulation of the list helps make the intellectual substance understandable. It is therefore faster. It makes the information units easier to comprehend. The facts are easier to compare to each other. Their number is apparent at first glance, whether they are numbered, bulleted or indented. As a result, information is presented more effectively, details are clearly ranked, data more accessible, and viewers can find what they are looking for faster.

The traditional text block
demanding effort
to read and study
to unearth the benefits
that are hidden in it.
Please read it
to find out
what the next
eight pages
are all about...

Write and design with color in mind

If you know before you start assembling your thoughts that color is going to be available, you can structure the organization of the writing to take advantage of the power that color can add to words in type. What you are about to read is an example. This version, written and displayed as running text, is the most common way of transmitting factual information. There's nothing wrong with it, but it does require concentrated study before the key points it contains are revealed. It is therefore slower than if it were written as a list, whose visible structure helps scanning. A list is a marriage of content with form, where the one cannot exist without the other. The very fact of its being seen as a list makes the information more inviting, because we know from experience that it will be quick and easy to take in. The visual tabulation of the list helps make the intellectual substance understandable. It is therefore faster. It makes the information units easier to comprehend. The facts are easier to compare to each other. Their number is apparent at first glance, whether they are numbered, bulleted or indented. As a result, information is presented more effectively, details are clearly ranked, data more accessible, and viewers can find what they are looking for faster.

This is the same as
the version on
the preceding page.
The information is hidden
in the text block.
The user must
search it out,
identify it,
and remember it.
That is a laborious
and time-consuming
process.

Write and design with color in mind

If you know before you start assembling your thoughts that color is going to be available, you can structure the organization of the writing to take advantage of the power that color can add to words in type. What you are about to read is an example. This version, written and displayed as running text, is the most common way of transmitting factual information. There's nothing wrong with it, but it does require concentrated study before the key points it contains are revealed. It is therefore slower than if it were written as a list, whose visible structure helps scanning. A list is a marriage of content with form, where the one cannot exist without the other. The very fact of its being seen as a list makes the information more inviting, because we know from experience that it will be quick and easy to take in. The visual tabulation of the list helps make the intellectual substance understandable. It is therefore faster. It makes the information units easier to comprehend. The facts are easier to compare to each other. Their number is apparent at first glance, whether they are numbered, bulleted or indented. As a result, information is presented more effectively, details are clearly ranked, data more accessible, and viewers can find what they are looking for faster.

How does red add value?
Not much.
Making the heading
or the box colorful
succeeds only in
making the heading
or the box colorful.
It is livelier than plain black,
but it adds no clues
to understanding
the message.

Write and design with color in mind

If you know before you start assembling your thoughts that color is going to be available, you can structure the organization of the writing to take advantage of the power that color can add to words in type. What you are about to read is an example. This version, written and displayed as running text, is the most common way of transmitting factual information. There's nothing wrong with it, but it does require concentrated study before the key points it contains are revealed. It is therefore slower than if it were written as a list, whose visible structure helps scanning. A list is a marriage of content with form, where the one cannot exist without the other. The very fact of its being seen as a list makes the information more inviting, because we know from experience that it will be quick and easy to take in. The visual tabulation of the list helps make the intellectual substance understandable. It is therefore faster. It makes the information units easier to comprehend. The facts are easier to compare to each other. Their number is apparent at first glance, whether they are numbered, bulleted or indented. As a result, information is presented more effectively, details are clearly ranked, data more accessible, and viewers can find what they are looking for faster.

A large block of text
run in color looks cheerful,
lively and attractive at first glance—
but it will go unread.
It is too uncomfortable to the eye.
Try it. You'll bog down by line 8.
When readers become conscious
of the act of reading,
they realize that they are "working"
and quickly stop.
The best type is "transparent."
By the way: notice how strong
the heading in black looks.

Write and design with color in mind

If you know before you start assembling your thoughts that color is going to be available, you can structure the organization of the writing to take advantage of the power that color can add to words in type. What you are about to read is an example. This version, written and displayed as running text, is the most common way of transmitting factual information. There's nothing wrong with it, but it does require concentrated study before the key points it contains are revealed. It is therefore slower than if it were written as a list, whose visible structure helps scanning. A list is a marriage of content with form, where the one cannot exist without the other. The very fact of its being seen as a list makes the information more inviting, because we know from experience that it will be quick and easy to take in. The visual tabulation of the list helps make the intellectual substance understandable. It is therefore faster. It makes the information units easier to comprehend. The facts are easier to compare to each other. Their number is apparent at first glance, whether they are numbered, bulleted or indented. As a result, information is presented more effectively, details are clearly ranked, data more accessible, and viewers can find what they are looking for faster.

The most hackneyed use of color:
tint-panel as background.
It is not "wrong."
It is just uninspiring.
If the purpose for its use
is to distinguish this material
from the other elements
on the page,
then, of course, it is succeeding,
and improving the message.
Be sure to make the color pale:
a 20% screen is maximum.

Write and design with color in mind

If you know before you start assembling your thoughts that color is going to be available, you can structure the organization of the writing to take advantage of the power that color can add to words in type. What you are about to read is an example. This version, written and displayed as running text, is the most common way of transmitting factual information. There's nothing wrong with it, but it does require concentrated study before the key points it contains are revealed. It is therefore slower than if it were written as a list, whose **visible structure helps scanning.** A list is a marriage of content with form, where the one cannot exist without the other. The very fact of its being seen as a list makes the **information more inviting**, because we know from experience that it will be quick and easy to take in. The visual tabulation of the list helps make the **intellectual substance understandable**. It is therefore **faster**. It makes the information units **easier to comprehend**. The **facts are easier to compare** to each other. Their **number is apparent** at first glance, whether they are numbered, bulleted or indented. As a result, **information is presented more effectively**, **details are clearly ranked**, **data more accessible**, and viewers can find what they are looking for faster.

The benefits contained
in the text
stand out in **boldface**.
Even in black-and-white,
a second tone of voice
has been added.
It speaks a little louder,
emphasizing those points
the reader is encouraged
to notice, because
they are the most important
and worthy of attention.

Write and design with color in mind

If you know before you start assembling your thoughts that color is going to be available, you can structure the organization of the writing to take advantage of the power that color can add to words in type. What you are about to read is an example. This version, written and displayed as running text, is the most common way of transmitting factual information. There's nothing wrong with it, but it does require concentrated study before the key points it contains are revealed. It is therefore slower than if it were written as a list, whose **visible structure helps scanning.** A list is a marriage of content with form, where the one cannot exist without the other. The very fact of its being seen as a list makes the **information more inviting**, because we know from experience that it will be quick and easy to take in. The visual tabulation of the list helps make the **intellectual substance understandable**. It is therefore **faster**. It makes the information units **easier to comprehend**. The **facts are easier to compare** to each other. Their **number is apparent** at first glance, whether they are numbered, bulleted or indented. As a result, **information is presented more effectively**, **details are clearly ranked**, **data more accessible**, and viewers can find what they are looking for faster.

Reversing the type
in white against
a color background
is so uncomfortable
for the eye to decipher,
that the difference
between the regular type
and the bold type
is hardly noticeable.
Nobody would bother
to read it anyway.

Write and design with color in mind

If you know before you start assembling your thoughts that color is going to be available, you can structure the organization of the writing to take advantage of the power that color can add to words in type. What you are about to read is an example. This version, written and displayed as running text, is the most common way of transmitting factual information. There's nothing wrong with it, but it does require concentrated study before the key points it contains are revealed. It is therefore slower than if it were written as a list, whose **visible structure helps scanning.** A list is a marriage of content with form, where the one cannot exist without the other. The very fact of its being seen as a list makes the **information more inviting**, because we know from experience that it will be quick and easy to take in. The visual tabulation of the list helps make the **intellectual substance understandable**. It is therefore **faster**. It makes the information units **easier to comprehend**. The **facts are easier to compare** to each other. Their **number is apparent** at first glance, whether they are numbered, bulleted or indented. As a result, **information is presented more effectively**, **details are clearly ranked**, **data more accessible**, and viewers can find what they are looking for faster.

Running the bold phrases in color,
turns the loud tone of voice into shouting.
This is the most obvious and expected
way of using color for emphasis.
But look how much paler
the red words are than the black ones.
They would hardly be visible
if they were not set in boldface.
Always bold the words to be run in color,
or make them a size larger
to compensate for the weakness of color
when compared to black.

Write and design with color in mind

If you know before you start assembling your thoughts that color is going to be available, you can structure the organization of the writing to take advantage of the power that color can add to words in type. What you are about to read is an example. This version, written and displayed as running text, is the most common way of transmitting factual information. There's nothing wrong with it, but it does require concentrated study before the key points it contains are revealed. It is therefore slower than if it were written as a list, whose **visible structure helps scanning.** A list is a marriage of content with form, where the one cannot exist without the other. The very fact of its being seen as a list makes the **information more inviting**, because we know from experience that it will be quick and easy to take in. The visual tabulation of the list helps make the **intellectual substance understandable**. It is therefore **faster**. It makes the information units **easier to comprehend**. The **facts are easier to compare** to each other. Their **number is apparent** at first glance, whether they are numbered, bulleted or indented. As a result, **information is presented more effectively**, **details are clearly ranked**, **data more accessible**, and viewers can find what they are looking for faster.

Notice how much more powerfully
the phrases in black
contrast against the type in color.
The mass of red type is less
difficult to accept,
when it is broken up
this way. Compare it to
the all-red version
on the last right-hand page
where the redness is
unrelieved by any contrasting
black words.

Write and design with color in mind

If you know before you start assembling your thoughts that color is going to be available, you can structure the organization of the writing to take advantage of the power that color can add to words in type. What you are about to read is an example. This version, was written and displayed as running text which is the most common way of transmitting factual information. There's nothing wrong with it, but it does require concentrated study before the key points it contains are revealed. It is therefore slower than if it were written as a list, whose visible structure helps scanning. A list is a marriage of content with form, where the one cannot exist without the other. By displaying it as a list,

- **Information is more inviting**, since the reader knows from experience that it will be quick and easy to take in.
- **Intellectual substance is more understandable** by its visual patterning as a menu.
- **Information is easier to comprehend** because it is segmented into units.
- **Facts are easy to compare** to each other.
- **The number of facts is available** at first glance.
- **Information is more effective** when facts are ranked clearly, and data are accessible.
- **Viewers find** what they are looking for faster.

The information is reworded
in itemized, bulleted list form.
Rewording created a parallel
verbal structure.
Its purpose: to make the material
immediately recognizeable as a list.
Lists are the fastest way
of presenting organized material.
Any organized verbal structure
can be displayed typographically.
A bulleted list is a format
the viewer accepts as "easy."

Write and design with color in mind

If you know before you start assembling your thoughts that color is going to be available, you can structure the organization of the writing to take advantage of the power that color can add to words in type. What you are about to read is an example. This version, was written and displayed as running text which is the most common way of transmitting factual information. There's nothing wrong with it, but it does require concentrated study before the key points it contains are revealed. It is therefore slower than if it were written as a list, whose visible structure helps scanning. A list is a marriage of content with form, where the one cannot exist without the other. By displaying it as a list,

- **Information is more inviting**, since the reader knows from experience that it will be quick and easy to take in.
- **Intellectual substance is more understandable** by its visual patterning as a menu.
- **Information is easier to comprehend** because it is segmented into units.
- **Facts are easy to compare** to each other.
- **The number of facts is available** at first glance.
- **Information is more effective** when facts are ranked clearly, and data are accessible.
- **Viewers find** what they are looking for faster.

The heading does indeed look
more attractive in red.
The bullets are undoubtedly
more decorative in red.
(They would look like green peas
if the color were green.)
But how does this color add
any intellectual value?
Decorating with color
like this has its place,
but it is no substitute
for logic.

Write and design with color in mind

If you know before you start assembling your thoughts that color is going to be available, you can structure the organization of the writing to take advantage of the power that color can add to words in type. What you are about to read is an example. This version, was written and displayed as running text which is the most common way of transmitting factual information. There's nothing wrong with it, but it does require concentrated study before the key points it contains are revealed. It is therefore slower than if it were written as a list, whose visible structure helps scanning. A list is a marriage of content with form, where the one cannot exist without the other. By displaying it as a list,

- **Information is more inviting**, since the reader knows from experience that it will be quick and easy to take in.
- **Intellectual substance is more understandable** by its visual patterning as a menu.
- **Information is easier to comprehend** because it is segmented into units.
- **Facts are easy to compare** to each other.
- **The number of facts is available** at first glance.
- **Information is more effective** when facts are ranked clearly, and data are accessible.
- **Viewers find** what they are looking for faster.

Letting the boldfaced bulleted items stand out in red gives them the requisite noticeability. Leaving the bullets black adds the decorative contrast achieved by the red bullets, opposite. Here they are part of the background rather than the foreground. They are outshouted by the words—which is the part that matters. Decoration in its proper place.

Write and design with color in mind

If you know before you start assembling your thoughts that color is going to be available, you can structure the organization of the writing to take advantage of the power that color can add to words in type. What you are about to read is an example. This version, was written and displayed as running text which is the most common way of transmitting factual information. There's nothing wrong with it, but it does require concentrated study before the key points it contains are revealed. It is therefore slower than if it were written as a list, whose visible structure helps scanning. A list is a marriage of content with form, where the one cannot exist without the other. By displaying it as a list,

- **Information is more inviting**, since the reader knows from experience that it will be quick and easy to take in.
- **Intellectual substance is more understandable** by its visual patterning as a menu.
- **Information is easier to comprehend** because it is segmented into units.
- **Facts are easy to compare** to each other.
- **The number of facts is available** at first glance.
- **Information is more effective** when facts are ranked clearly, and data are accessible.
- **Viewers find** what they are looking for faster.

Alternate version, swapping red for black in the text. The important phrases in black stand out much more visibly. The black bullets belong to them.

Write and design with color in mind

If you know before you start assembling your thoughts that color is going to be available, you can structure the organization of the writing to take advantage of the power that color can add to words in type. What you are about to read is an example. This version was written and displayed as running text, which is the most common way of transmitting factual information. There's nothing wrong with it, but it does require concentrated study before the key points it contains are revealed. It is therefore slower than if it were written as a list, whose visible structure helps scanning. A list is a marriage of content with form, where the one cannot exist without the other.

Listing information is visually beneficial

It encourages scanning by the way it is structured

It reveals the extent of coverage at first glance

It makes information accessible by its display

It explains substance by its own patterning

It facilitates comprehension by separating facts

It allows comparison of facts to each other

It ranks details by the way they are exhibited

It presents data more efficiently by tabulation

It helps viewers find what they are looking for

The second half of the text
is rewritten and composed as a list
with the benefits shouted
as the first active words in each line.
Each element is edited down to
a concise, single-line statement.
The content makes use of visual form.
The generous line spacing makes
bullets unnecessary, specially when
all items are single-liners.
The new subhead announces
and defines the list's purpose.

Write and design with color in mind

If you know before you start assembling your thoughts that color is going to be available, you can structure the organization of the writing to take advantage of the power that color can add to words in type. What you are about to read is an example. This version was written and displayed as running text, which is the most common way of transmitting factual information. There's nothing wrong with it, but it does require concentrated study before the key points it contains are revealed. It is therefore slower than if it were written as a list, whose visible structure helps scanning. A list is a marriage of content with form, where the one cannot exist without the other.

Listing information is visually beneficial

It encourages scanning by the way it is structured

It reveals the extent of coverage at first glance

It makes information accessible by its display

It explains substance by its own patterning

It facilitates comprehension by separating facts

It allows comparison of facts to each other

It ranks details by the way they are exhibited

It presents data more efficiently by tabulation

It helps viewers find what they are looking for

Popping out the heading
and the subhead in color
is pretty, but not very significant.
The color does not help to bring
the message to the viewer's
eyes or consciousness.
Nor does it hinder it.
It is just intellectually
under-used.

Write and design with color in mind

If you know before you start assembling your thoughts that color is going to be available, you can structure the organization of the writing to take advantage of the power that color can add to words in type. What you are about to read is an example. This version was written and displayed as running text, which is the most common way of transmitting factual information. There's nothing wrong with it, but it does require concentrated study before the key points it contains are revealed. It is therefore slower than if it were written as a list, whose visible structure helps scanning. A list is a marriage of content with form, where the one cannot exist without the other.

Listing information is visually beneficial

It encourages scanning by the way it is structured
It reveals the extent of coverage at first glance
It makes information accessible by its display
It explains substance by its own patterning
It facilitates comprehension by separating facts
It allows comparison of facts to each other
It ranks details by the way they are exhibited
It presents data more efficiently by tabulation
It helps viewers find what they are looking for

The second line of the title,
the new subhead,
and the list of benefits
are shown in red
to distinguish them from
the rest of the material,
and to make them noticeable.
Color illuminates
the important parts.
The result:
less work,
faster comprehension
correct interpretation.

Write and design with color in mind

If you know before you start assembling your thoughts that color is going to be available, you can structure the organization of the writing to take advantage of the power that color can add to words in type. What you are about to read is an example. This version was written and displayed as running text, which is the most common way of transmitting factual information. There's nothing wrong with it, but it does require concentrated study before the key points it contains are revealed. It is therefore slower than if it were written as a list, whose visible structure helps scanning. A list is a marriage of content with form, where the one cannot exist without the other.

Listing information is visually beneficial

It encourages scanning by the way it is structured
It reveals the extent of coverage at first glance
It makes information accessible by its display
It explains substance by its own patterning
It facilitates comprehension by separating facts
It allows comparison of facts to each other
It ranks details by the way they are exhibited
It presents data more efficiently by tabulation
It helps viewers find what they are looking for

The reverse of the scheme at left.
The black stands out more strongly
than the red.
However, this version runs counter
to the readers' expectations,
since the colored elements
are assumed to be the important ones.
There is just too much color
and here it is applied
to the wrong material.
Is there a "correct" solution? No.
It is all a matter of interpretation,
balance, and purpose.

Example 2: ***Telephone list, before***

The document's own design gets in the way and impedes its usefulness. It draws attention away from the information and directs it towards itself. The time and effort spent in embroidering it with borders, shadow-boxes, bullets, stars, clip art, inconsistent and illogical typographic arrangement, and even bad spelling would have been better spent analyzing its purpose.

HELP NUMBERS

Customer Support Center (7th Floor Wing A) Extension 5000

- IMPSROD Down
- All Hardware Problems
- Envoy Problems
- Host Problems
- Main Frame Output Questions
- Abends
- Stuck on Clock/ Response Time
- Restricted/Revoked/Forgotten Password

Office Systems (14th Floor Central Building) Extension 4010

- All PC Software
- DataEase
- Displaywrite
- WordPerfect
- Host Emulation Software
- Problems Printing From Your PC
- Lotus
- Harvard Graphics
- PC DOS

★ ✻✻ ★

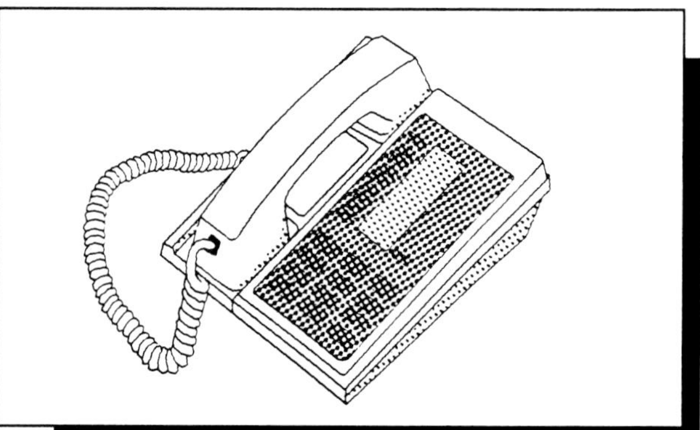

NOTE:
BROKEN PC TERMINAL'S, PRINTER'S, MONITOR'S, PC'S, ETC CALL EXT 5000. THEY IN TURN CALL OUTSIDE THE COMPANY.

☞ YOU ☞

Are Responsible For Accurately And Professionally Describing The Severity Level To Your Contact

The purpose of the document is to tell the user which of two extensions to call for help with computer problems. It must be easy to read, fast to scan, with type large enough to discern when the paper is hanging on the tackboard over there.

Thoughts are rammed into arbitrary patterns dictated by line length, not by sense. Two columns are too narrow to allow each item to read as a single line and forces short turnovers.

The focal points for the piece (the extension numbers) are hard to find at the end of the sentences.

Embellishing the picture and filling the space with decorative pimples, adds nothing to the directness and understandability of the piece.

Telephone list, after

The type is shaped to expose the significance of the message.
One glimpse and the meaning jumps off the page:

- rank 1: HELP, 5000 and 4010
- rank 2: lists of problems applicable to each number
- rank 3: two footnotes

The red items are exposed in white space, to give them maximal noticeability. That is why the basic layout is deliberately off-center. Using color cleverly is as much a matter of the space in which it is presented, as of the choice of thoughts it is used to spotlight—or in which typeface and typesize they will be set.

Space is used judiciously, not wasted on framing... whatever is left can be larger, more powerful.

Each thought is given a single line, fostering fast comprehension.

Type is used to categorize the information: Franklin Gothic for telephone-oriented facts. Garamond for user-oriented problems. Tiny type for footnotes.

Help numbers

IMSPROD down
All hardware problems
Envoy problems
Host problems
Mainframe output questions
Abends
Stuck on clock, response time
Restricted, revoked, forgotten passwords

X 5000 **CUSTOMER SUPPORT CENTER (7th FLOOR, WING A)**

All PC software
DataEase
Displaywrite
WordPerfect
Host emulation software
Problems printing from your PC
Lotus
Harvard Graphics
PC DOS

X 4010 **OFFICE SYSTEMS (14th FLOOR, CENTRAL BUILDING)**

Broken PC terminals, printers, monitors, PCs, etc. call ext. 5000. They, in turn, call outside the Company.

You are responsible for describing accurately and professionally the severity level to your contact.

Example 3: **Newsletter, before**

The original version of this appalling disaster has only been changed to hide the names of the perpetrators.
The underlying problem: seeing each item as a separate bit, unrelated to its neighbors.
Refusing to see the page as an entity turns it into a wastebasket of odds-and-ends.
The lack of coordination results in exaggerations, in order to make various parts noticeable.
Space (i.e. paper) is reduced to fallow impotent background.

Helping You Find The Right Combination For Successful Cooperation

A NEWSLETTER FROM THE ***ASSOCIATION FOR GETTING MORE DONE***

FEBRUARY 1795 **VOLUME 17** **NO. 2**

Study Shows Management Can Improve Output

From Our Special Correspondent

Recent years have shown how important it is for the management team that organizes work flow to pay attention to the wishes and preferences of the people who are actually going to be faced with doing the work they get paid to do, (though everyone agrees that the rate of remuneration for such labor is not merely laughable but insulting) if output is ever to exceed the attainable goals set in the previous five-year-plans and which have been frustrated over

(continued on page 4)

Photo by Christopher Valerian

Knotty problem symbolizes complexity facing the Normal Organization's management.

AAPGTM: Inevitable Need for Compliance Next FY

Editor's Note: This is the second and last of a series of articles on the subject of the AAPGTM.

In this article, which is the second and last of a series in which we will be considering the AAPGTM and its effect on the working conditions of the typical working employee in organizations of over 250 employees, we will have to face the fact that the Government has called for 100% compliance by the and of the current fiscal year. This is going to create difficulties for many organizations who have to fulfill the needs of their own production schedules while simultaneously looking toward the success of their bottom lines and the satisfaction

(Continued on Page 4)

Inside

The self-conscious nameplate (or logo) is buried by competing words that crackle like visual static.

The rule above the date and volume number is a torture rack to stretch them on, poor things.

Centering the headline is the weakest way to give it attention—as is the lightness of type. Smaller and bolder is more effective. Three more words, too!

Since nothing aligns, nothing belongs. Besides, it looks messy.

Caption overplays the photo credit, and revels in that awful widow: "gement." This is not well crafted. It does not inspire confidence in the viewer/reader, who is tempted to think: *"Humph, if they are satisfied with this sort of mess, it is likely that their message is just as shoddy."*

Bold rule to divide elements should not be necessary. It just adds more ink.

The box is an oversized out-of-scale intrusion.

Upper-and-lower case of heads is harder to read than all lowercase. Look how much more aggressive and uglier it is, too.

Newsletter, after

Direct, accessible information: *Who is it? What's the big news? What's secondary?*
This is not the result of theoretical aesthetics but of practical work: defining information-units.
The items are organized into self-contained, rectangular, recognizeable groups.
Space is tightened within each unit, but broad moats separate the groups from each other.
Typography is simplified, because excessive variety is not merely unnecessary, but distracting.

The logo stands out in both boldness (nothing is stronger than good old black) and in its clearly-defined space. The supporting slogan belongs to the logo but does not compete.

Color panel separates the organization's material, while defining the logo area.

Half-pica narrower text columns are shunted to the right, leaving a swath of space at left into which headlines extend for more visual power.

Crucial paragraph of copy is picked out in color. That is why it is set in boldface. Notice, too, that the lead story is set a size larger than the secondary story.

Caption (or legend) is lightened up, but a boldface lead-in attracts the eye. Photo credit is pulled over to the side.

AAPTGM acronym picked out in black for emphasis, rest of head is paler in color.

Editor's note is set in italics, ragged-right, to separate it from the story proper. Note that there are eight more text lines than in the original.

Continued line is tied into the text.

Table of contents is differentiated from the news by colored panel and type. The look is an immediate clue to their dissimilarity.

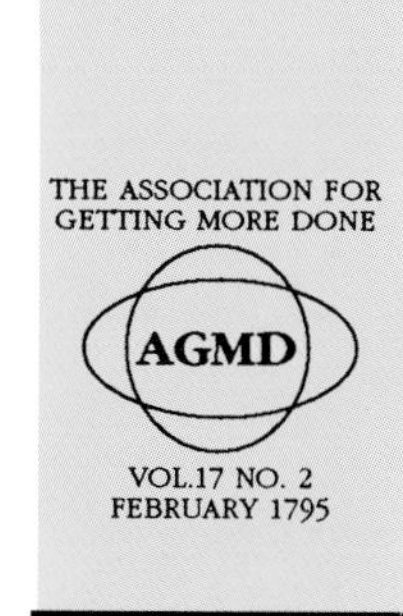

THE ASSOCIATION FOR GETTING MORE DONE
AGMD
VOL.17 NO. 2
FEBRUARY 1795

WORKING TOGETHER

HELPING YOU FIND THE RIGHT COMBINATION FOR SUCCESSFUL COOPERATION

Study shows management could start improving output immediately

From our special correspondent

Recent years have shown how important it is for the management team that organizes work flow to pay attention to the wishes and preferences of the people who are actually going to be faced with doing the work they get paid to do, **(though everyone agrees that the rate of remuneration for such labor is not merely laughable but insulting)** if output is ever to exceed the attainable goals set in the previous five-year-plans and which have been frustrated over *(continued on page 4)*

Photo by Christopher Valerian

***Knotty problem** symbolizes complexity facing the normal organization's management*

AAPGTM: Inevitable need for compliance next FY

Editor's Note:
This is the second and last of a series of articles on the subject of the AAPGTM.

In this article, which is the second and last of a series in which we will be considering the AAPGTM and its effect on the working conditions of the typical working employee in organizations of over 250 employees, we will have to face the fact that the Government has called for 100% compliance by the and of the current fiscal year. This is going to create difficulties for many organizations who have to fulfill the needs of their own production schedules while simultaneously looking toward the success of their bottom lines and the satisfaction of the shareholders. The text had ended just before the word shareholders. All this copy is added to the original. You have to stop wasting space on the wrong stuff: too many useless spaces between things and type too pale and too large. It works.

Inside

Example 4: **Inter-office memo, before**

What's wrong with it? Nothing—and everything.
It is typical of its kind: unimaginative and unresponsive to the reader's needs.
The sender assumes the recipient will welcome its arrival and bother to study it.
Would **you**?

ATTENTION REGISTRATION COORDINATORS

FEE RATE INCREASES EFFECTIVE 01 / 01 / 95

1) $60.00 Examination Fee For All Registered Representative Examinations.

2) $75.00 Examination Fee For All Registered Principal Examinations.

3) $15.00 Fee For Printing Fingerprints.

Begin submitting these increased fees by the date on which increases are scheduled.

EXAMINATION WAITING PERIOD

Effective November 31 1994, Candidates who fail an NARPM examination must wait thirty (30) days before the examination can be retaken. After the third and subsequent attempts, the Representative must wait one hundred-and-eighty (180) days between examinations. NOTE: This does not apply to the Series 10097.4R-PM examination, as it is only administered on a monthly basis.

TRANSFER-FORM REQUIREMENTS

Effective September 01 / 94, the NARPM requires Employers to provide TERMINATING employees with a copy of the filed MP-5/0J. Therefore we are now required to obtain a copy of MP-5/0J from the most recent employer on TRANSFERRED employees. Please submit the MP-5/01J together with the MP-4/0J, 12-47 and all other Employee Registration Forms.

STATE REGULATION CHANGES

MN: Fee Changes Effective November 31 / 93: Registration $30.00. Renewal $ 30.00. Transfer $30.00

GA: The October 21 Series 10097.4 RPM Examinations Will Be Held at the Ramada Inn Southwest, I-85 and Saugatuck Road, 13500 SW Expwy, Atlanta.

---

cc: Administrative Supervisor

The two segments of the head (Attention! Who?) look the same, with Cute But Useless Typographic Embellishment. Monotonous.

Headings are pale and wan, illegible because they are in all-caps, hidden because they are centered and no bolder than the text type.

Overall blandness of emphasis. Nothing stands out. Each item looks equally important.

Looks untidy because spaces between elements vary.

Dashed rules add complexity. More ink on the page does not necessarily make it better.

Hard to read, because lines are much too long.

Arbitrary and inconsistent use of all-caps in some words, capitalized initials in others.

Dark type makes it dingy and depressing.

Inter-office memo, after

The target audience is alerted to its special concerns by boldness, size and placement. It is easy to scan, and reads better, faster. (Text was also edited to be less stilted.) Color has been used to add first-glance value: it is the visual clue that prompts those to whom the message is addressed to pay attention to that one critical item you want them to notice first.

Two-level reading is encouraged: the viewer scans the heads, can skip uninteresting or subsidiary matter.

Type used in titles contrasts against text. Text lines are shorter for greater legibility.

Ragged-right setting is more informal, reader-friendly.

The color is effective because of its contrast to the surrounding black. The less color, the more special it is, and the more striking the contrast.

The text type run in color is a bolder version of the text face, to make sure that it is as legible as if it were black. This is Futura, which is bolder than Futura Light used for the other text blocks. Heads are in Futura Bold.

The casual viewer's curiosity is piqued by the color. The piece looks special. It demands to be noticed.

Attention **registration coordinators**

Rate increases for examination fees

Effective January 1, 1995, please submit the following fees:

$ 60.00 for all registered representative exams
$ 75.00 for all registered principal exams
$ 15.00 for fingerprinting

Examination waiting periods

Effective November 31 1994, candidates who fail an NARPM exam must wait 30 days before retaking the examination.
After the third attempt, the waiting period is 180 days.
(This does not apply to Series 10097.4R-PM exams, administered monthly.)

Transfer-form requirements

Effective September 1, 1994, NARPM requires employers to provide terminating employees with a copy of their filed MP-5OJ. We are now required to obtain a copy of this form from the most recent employer on transferred employees. Please submit it with the MP-4/QJ, 12-47 and other registration forms.

State regulation changes and announcements

MN: Registration, renewal, and transfer fees will be increased to $30.00 as of November 31 1993.

GA: The October 21, 1993 Series 10097.4 RPM examinations will be held at Ramada Inn Southwest, I-85 and Saugatuck Road, 13500 SW Expwy, Atlanta.

cc: Administrative Supervisor

Example 5: **Policy cover, before**

Policies are expected to be unresponsive and impossible to read. Their unfriendly reputation is well deserved: they have been written and assembled for the company's, not the recipient's, convenience. Suspicious customers worry about "the small type."
They must be humanized—but this example assumes that the language is legally sacred, and only its form is malleable. Can such a grey mass be made penetrable?

"Life is for Living"

THE ESURIENT INSURANCE COMPANY

A Mutual Company Incorporated in 1867

Home Office: Esurient Tower, Westbury, Connecticut

Name of Insured Polonius H. MacBeth | 42 Age of Insured

Face Amount $ 5,000,000.00 | February 30, 1994 Policy Date

Policy Number FPAL 000-35-67859 | June 31,1994 Date of Issue

FLEXIBLE PREMIUM ADJUSTABLE LIFE INSURANCE POLICY

Adjustable Death Benefit Payable At Death Prior To Maturity Date -- See Death Benefit On Page 6.
Cash Values Equal To Or Greater Than Those Required By Law
Maturity Proceeds, If Any, Payable On Maturity Date
Flexible Premiums Payable To Maturity Date Or Prior Death
THIS IS A NON-PARTICIPATING POLICY AND IS NOT ELIGIBLE FOR DIVIDENDS

WE AGREE to pay the death proceeds to the Beneficiary if the Insured dies before Maturity Date and while this policy is in force. We agree to pay any maturity proceeds to you if the Insured is living on the Maturity Date and this policy is in force.These agreements are subject to the terms of this policy.

PLEASE READ this policy carefully. It is a legal contract between you and our company.

NOTICE OF TWENTY DAY RIGHT to examine this policy. It is important to us that you are satisfied with this policy. You have 20 days after you receive it to decide if it meets with your needs. If you are not satisfied, you may return the policy to us or to our agent. If the policy is received or postmarked before midnight of the 20th day after it was delivered to you, we will cancel it and any premiums paid will be refunded.

SIGNED FOR the *Esurient Insurance Company* of Westbury, Connecticut, on the Date of Issue.

PRESIDENT | SECRETARY

Four segments of information must be accommodated:
- Who are we, the company?
- Who are you?
- What is it about?
- What do we contract to do?

Here they swim into each other... but that does not matter: after all, we The Company, are familiar with this material and know what we are looking at and what it is for, and the form is for us, not you.

The customer needs the segments demarcated. Each segment must also be easy to read, at the very least.

Look at the self-important upper-and-lowercasing of the text: it is nearly as off-putting as the ridiculously long lines of tiny type that are so unfriendly as to inhibit anyone but the most dedicated from reading them. The suspicion grows: maybe the company is not anxious to have this material understood? Obviously that is not the intention. Yet the visual presentation carries that subtle implication which creates the wrong impression in the one person who should be happy and comfortable: the customer.

Policy cover, after

The information is broken into units, separated by space and rules. The Insured's data is concentrated in a quick-scan list. All available vertical space is used, to allow lines to be shorter. And color helps the customers find what they want to know immediately: Who is this document from... whom is it for... what is it about... what's-in-it-for-me?

The list of subjects of the agreement is highlighted. This is what the customer is buying.

The logo is filled with color—since the available color happens to match the company's standard hue. If it does not match exactly, it is better to use a neutral pale grey, and reserve color to draw attention to the elements that are more important than identification: the customer's concerns.

The rules and box give structure to the page and define the four elements it contains

Type details are simpler, clearer, giving greater contrast to those parts that need to be emphasized.

Variable information, such as the name, age etc stand out: a flattering gesture making Mr.McBeth feel as though the Company cared for him as an individual, (which they may well do). It is good business for all concerned to make that attitude obvious.

"*Life is for Living*"

THE ESURIENT
INSURANCE
COMPANY

A MUTUAL COMPANY INCORPORATED IN 1867
HOME OFFICE: ESURIENT TOWER, WESTBURY, CONNECTICUT

Name of insured : Polonius H. McBeth
Age of insured : 42
Face amount : $5,000,000.00
Policy date : February 30,1994
Policy number : FPAL 000-35-67859
Date of issue : June 31,1994

FLEXIBLE PREMIUM ADJUSTABLE LIFE INSURANCE POLICY
Adjustable death benefit payable at death prior to maturity date. (See Death benefit on page 6.)
Cash values equal to or greater than those required by law.
Maturity proceeds, if any, payable on maturity date.
Flexible premiums payable to maturity date or prior death
This is a non-participating policy and is not eligible for dividends.

We agree to pay the death proceeds to the beneficiary if the insured dies before maturity date and while this policy is in force. We agree to pay any maturity proceeds to you if the insured is living on the maturity date and this policy is in force.These agreements are subject to the terms of this policy.

Please read this policy carefully. It is a legal contract between you and our company.

Notice of twenty-day right to examine this policy. It is important to us that you are satisfied with this policy. You have twenty days after you receive it to decide if it meets with your needs. If you are not satisfied, you may return the policy to us or to our agent. If the policy is received or postmarked before midnight of the twentieth day after it was delivered to you, we will cancel it and any premiums paid will be refunded.

Signed for Esurient Insurance Company of Westbury, Connecticut, on the date of issue.

President   Secretary

EK 00-30.87125.9

Example 6: ***Flyer, before***

Invitation to attend a convention: is it a professional occasion or a chance for whoopee?
First impression: what a mess—can it be valuable to one's career?
Second impression: why is the future looking so depressing? (Look at the graph).
Third impression: is this organization's thinking as crude and primitive as it is here represented?
Resulting worry: is this piece doing justice to the organization that sent it out?

NHLMA

10th ANNUAL CONFERENCE

FEBRUARY 29-31, 1994

THE OSTENTIA-MAJESTIC & AUTOCHTON HOTELS, PIERIA, ML.

ESSENTIALS OF FINANCIAL MANAGEMENT
ELECTRONIC PAYMENT
INVESTMENT MANAGEMENT SYSTEMS
BORROWING VS INVESTMENT
INTERNATIONAL TOPICS
CAPITAL MARKETS
CONTEMPORARY FINANCIAL MANAGEMENT
REGULATORY SUBJECTS
CAREER DEVELOPMENT
FINANCIAL PRICING/SERVICES
COLLECTIONS SYSTEMS
MONETARY FORECASTING

FOCUS

RISK!

PAYMENT SYSTEMS
NON-CREDIT SERVICES
INTEREST RATES
MARKET
CREDIT
FOREIGN EXCHANGE

NATIONAL HYPOTHETICAL LUCRE MANAGEMENT ASSOCIATION

A NON-PROFIT PROFESSIONAL ORGANIZATION

Three elements make up this confusing image:
1. Who are we?
2. What's happening?
3. Why should you bother to attend—what's in it for you?
They are all muddled and intertwined together.

Instead of clarifying the groups of ideas, to make the piece not only inviting but persuasive, it has been decorated and "laid out" with superficial embellishment.

The symbolic graph interrupts and appears to point downwards—to failure.

The word FOCUS is inside a symbolic magnifying glass that emphasizes the wrong concept: it isn't the focus that matters but rather subject of Risk.

And the word RISK is at a funny angle because the computer can do it.

The seminar subjects are set in illegible all-caps, boxed into an arbitrary pattern.

Upshot: the viewer is not guided by the piece, but is left to hop and skip around trying to make head or tail of this insult. It is all based on the arrogant assumption that the recipients will be so intrigued that they will not mind wasting their precious time deciphering it.

Flyer, after

The organization's name and function are identified with dignity.
The event is identified, dated, and located at first glance.
The details are easily scanned.
The special (risk-related) subjects highlighted.

The white space is not neutral background, but used to separate the units of information from each other. Its "empty, wasted" areas are foils for the "full, used" ones

A single and more elegant type has been used. The strong contrast of size not only looks compelling, but also makes sense.

See the difference in style between the type used for the logo and corporate identity material, and the rest of the message. They are two different things, so it makes sense to make them look different.

NHLMA

NATIONAL HYPOTHETICAL LUCRE MANAGEMENT ASSOCIATION

A NON-PROFIT PROFESSIONAL ORGANIZATION

Tenth annual conference

The Ostentia-Majestic
and
Autochton Hotels
Pieria, ML.
February 29-31, 1994

- Essentials of financial management
- Electronic payment
- Investment management systems
- Borrowing vs. investment
- International topics
- Capital markets
- Contemporary financial management
- Regulatory subjects
- Career development
- Financial pricing/services
- Collections systems
- Monetary forecasting

Focus: risk

- Payment systems
- Non-credit services
- Interest rates
- Market
- Credit
- Foreign exchange

Example 7: **Work schedule, before**

Here is a simple presentation of related facts: a sequence of ten actions or events coordinated with the thirteen weeks scheduled for their completion.
Its purpose: a quick overview. Word-processing equipment limits type size and line weight to monotonous grey, and thus the tone of voice with which the piece speaks.

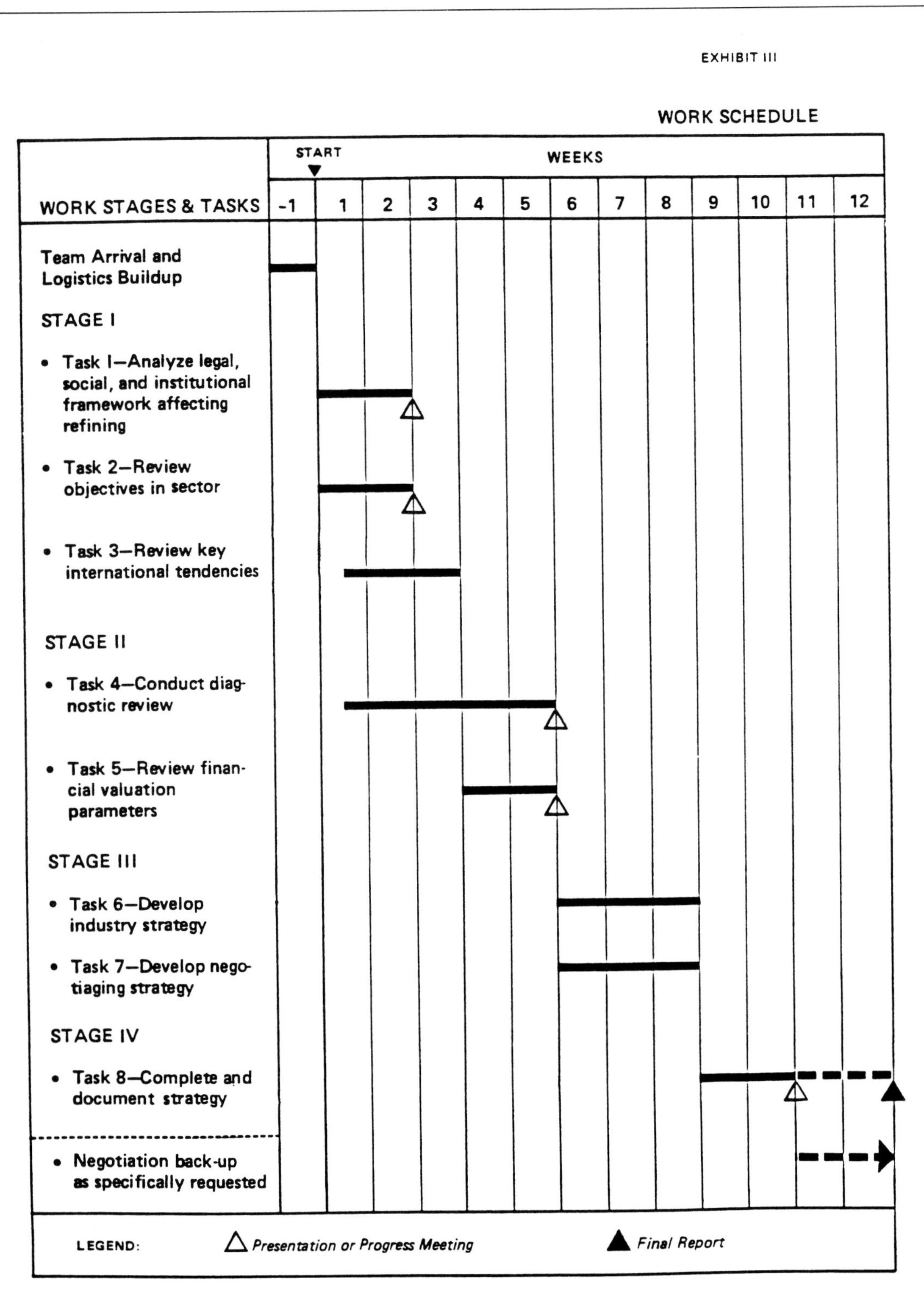

What is this? The title and Exhibit III line are not noticeable at first glance.

The list of actions, broken into stages and tasks, is nigh on indecipherable without careful concentration and analysis. The bullets add no clues. They just indicate the fact that this is a list. That fact is obvious from the material itself, so they are superfluous.

The space devoted to the diagram is wider than its simple substance needs, and so the text is squeezed into a column that is too narrow. That is why the information contained in the text is not visibly tabulated, but is, instead, a heavy reading-job.

The handling lacks finesse, imagination, emphasis, or visual expressiveness that can guide the viewer through the raw data to understanding its implications. That is what is meant by "boring."

Work schedule, after

The redesign tabulates the written information for clear oversight. Condensed type leaves ample room to accommodate the diagram. Color is used to define the special area of interest to one segment of the audience. It is highlighted so they not only notice it immediately, but also are guided to follow the visual and intellectual sequence from left to right and upward, or the other way round.

What did you look at first? Chances are that it was the information in the red area:

Review financial valuation parameters.

Then your eye moved toward the right and up to Week 4 and 5.

The color separates the information that is specific to a small group of readers, or of greater value than the other information.

An alternate technique which is probably more effective: reverse the areas: make the surroundings blue, and let the L-shape stand out in white. The type in black on white will gain legibility because of the strong contrast of black-to-white, in comparison to the harder to read black-on-blue.

Compare details of typographic style changes between the Before and After. Their purpose: simplify the image the viewer sees.

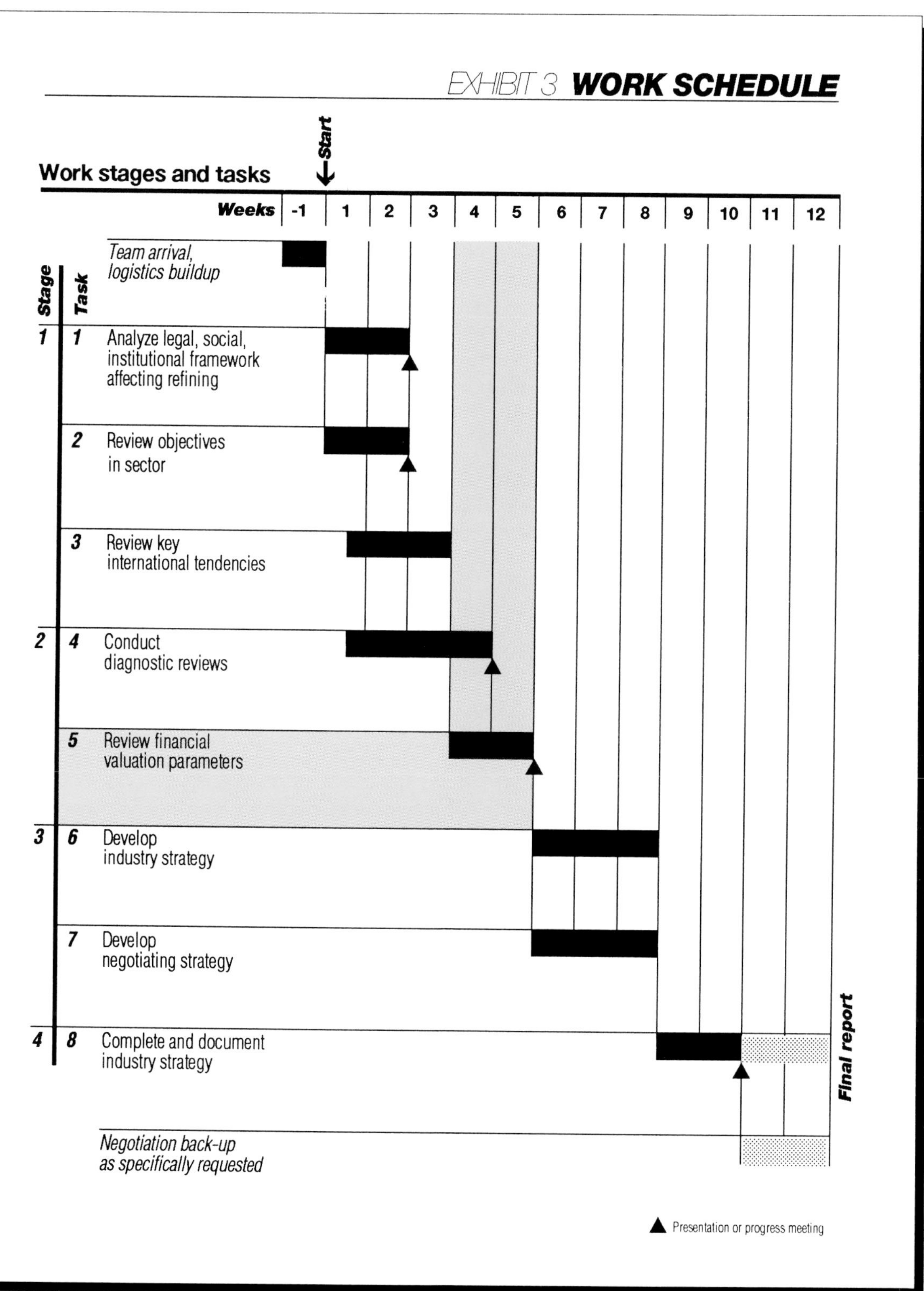

Example 8: **Poster, before**

A simple list of bulleted items needs to be made important and highly visible.
The text is split into units, each item placed in its own casket.
The coffins are stacked up the middle of the page. The very large size of the very wide type in boxes that are too short forces some phrases into two lines which read badly and look worse.

GATEKEEPING GUIDELINES

- Be open to and encourage ideas
- Look for merit in the ideas
- Strive for win-win situation
- Listen non-defensively
- Pay attention, avoid side conversations
- Limit war stories
- Look for facts
- Help to summarize
- Be responsible for team's progress

Poster, after

A large area of color is stronger than a cluster of little ones.
Its very size helps to attract the eye, especially if the color is friendly and cheerful.
Ramped color guides the viewer smoothly downward from the heading to the individual items.
Color helps to fulfill the poster's purpose of inspiring and instructing.

Breaking the fifth item into two makes each short enough to fit into one line.

Using a condensed type makes lines shorter, so words fit into the space. Using a bolder version of the face makes the message stronger.

Separating the units with hairlines creates dramatic contrast of light to dark.

Making the hairlines the same width ties them to the bold rule above the title.

The deep indent of the text creates a space up the left-hand edge which acts as a foil to the first part of the word "Gatekeeping." That, as well as the moat of space beneath it, helps it stand out and gives it the dignity and power that a heading needs.

Unimaginative and hackneyed bullets have been replaced by a more cheerful decorative symbol.

Gatekeeping guidelines

- **Be open and encourage ideas**
- **Look for merit in the ideas**
- **Strive for win-win situation**
- **Listen non-defensively**
- **Pay attention**
- **Avoid side conversations**
- **Limit war stories**
- **Look for facts**
- **Help to summarize**
- **Be responsible for team's progress**

13 Technicalities about color

What is color? All cows look black at night because there is no light. Color is an effect created by light. Where there is no light, there is no color.

Light is a form of energy traveling in waves. It is part of the electromagnetic spectrum which consists of waves of different lengths. Only a small group of them are visible to humans. The invisible ones are radio waves, microwaves, X-rays and so on. The spectrum of visible ones—"white" light—is composed of a rainbow of color bands: red, orange, yellow, green, blue, indigo, violet. (That is what Sir Isaac Newton proved when he refracted a beam of white light through a prism.)

Each color of the visible spectrum has its own wavelength. We respond to those ranging from red (long, 700 nanometers) to violet (short, about 360 nm). Wavelengths combined in correct proportions produce white light. White light contains all visible colors.

Each individual sees differently and therefore the interpretation of color, like beauty, is in the eye of the beholder. The physiology of color perception is not yet fully understood and measuring individual interpretation is an inexact science. Abnormal vision is easier to define. 8% of men but only 1% of women are color-deficient to some degree, usually red/green. But it is also a proven fact that peoples' sensitivity to yellow increases in winter. It then changes to sensitivity to green in summer. Further to complicate matters, sensitivity to color decreases with age in most individuals. So we are dealing with an obscure and variable factor.

The colors we perceive depend on the strength and mixture of wavelengths striking the receptors in our eyes. The incoming light is transformed into neural impulses by the cones and rods that make up the receptors. The 6 milion *cones* are concentrated towards the center of the retina. They are responsible for sharp vision and color perception. Nearly two-thirds of them contain photopigments sensitive to red lightwaves, one-third to green, and a few (2%) to blue/violet. They are surrounded by 120 million *rods* which are sensitive to black-and-white and help us see in the dark. The impulses travel to the brain through the *optic nerve*.

The brain interprets the impulses from various combinations of red, green, and blue/violet as "colors." Red and green stimulated together, for instance, produce the effect of yellow. The physical way in which the eye works makes some colors easier to see than others. There are also some combinations of hues and values that irritate the eye and are therefore unpleasant and tiring.

Since the retina is sensitive to red and green in the center, with grey and blue around the periphery, it is wise to place the most important element in the center and use red and green there, especially in slides and displays. If you put red or green elements on the periphery, draw additional attention to them by increasing their size, using a blinking light, placing amusing cartoon symbols there, etc. By the same token, blue or grey are successful background field colors precisely because those are colors that react equally throughout the eye. For that reason, it is unwise to run text or small details in blue.

To be discerned most vividly, shape and color should blend and work together. Eyes tend to notice the edges of what they are looking at. The edges, in turn, bring the image into focus. We also recognize objects by their outline, their contours. It is not certain whether this is an innate human characteristic or whether it is accultured, but when you draw a dog or a house, you—and just about everybody else—draws the outline. The shape is the recognizeable icon that symbolizes the object. Color helps to define elements most effectively when the edge of its shape is clearly demarcated from its neighbor and, simultaneously, clearly differs from it in both hue and value.

Color is only reflected Objects have no color of their own. A cucumber appears green to us because it absorbs all the light waves that strike it *except the green ones*. Those it reflects and they bounce into our eyes and so we say "what a beautiful green ripe cucumber." All solid objects have their particular color because they reflect only the wavelengths corresponding to that color and absorb all the others. In a sense, color is actually a "rejected" material. It is wasted, and white most of all: objects look white because they reflect all wavelengths equally.

Limeade appears green to us for the same reasons, despite the fact that it is not solid. The light passes through the liquid, and all wavelengths except green are absorbed. Only the green wavelength is transmitted through and by it to our eyes, so we see refreshing, cool limeade.

Additive color (RGB) Colors produced by light energy are *additive*. The source of light (the sun, lightbulb, candle etc) is the source of additive energy. The more colors are added, the lighter the image becomes until pure white light appears—if the colors are in balance.

The *primary colors* of the visible spectrum are ***R***ed, ***G***reen, and ***B***lue/violet. They are called primary, because all other colors can be produced by combining or adding them in various proportions. The colors seen on your monitor's CRT tube are additive. They are created by bombarding three kinds of phosphorus (red, green and blue/violet) with an electron beam.

Combining the three primaries in certain proportions produces white.

Combining two primaries produces a *secondary*:
Red and blue/violet produce magenta.
Green and blue/violet produce cyan.
Green and red produce yellow.

Subtractive color (CMY) Colors produced by subtracting energy are *subtractive*. Color reflected by an object is subtractive because it absorbs (i.e. subtracts) all the wavelengths from the light that hits it except the ones which it reflects and which distinguish the object and makes us see the cucumber as being green.

Pigments, paints, toners, printing inks are all "subtractive." The more colors are added, the darker the image, until black is produced.

The subtractive colors of the process printing inks (CMYK) are picked and balanced to match the additive colors:
Cyan is made of blue/violet and green (and absorbs red)
Magenta is made of red and blue/violet (and absorbs green)
Yellow is made of red and green (and absorbs blue/violet)

Combining two secondaries produces the *tertiary* color they share::
Cyan plus yellow create green.
Magenta plus yellow create red.
Magenta plus cyan create blue/violet.

K: blac***K*** is added to the C, M, and Y in process printing to add definition to details and strengthen shadow areas. K is used to avoid confusing* it with "Blue" sometimes used instead of the word "cyan."

* Is it ***CMYK*** or ***YMCK***?
CMYK is the sequence in which most desktop programs work.
YMCK is the sequence in which designers and printers have traditionally worked, because it is the normal sequence in which process colors are laid down on press.
Both are right.

Dimensions of color Color has three "dimensions" or characteristics:

1. Hue: the basic color of the color. Its redness, blueness, greenness. Every color has its dominant wavelength which gives it its brownness, pinkness, purpleness.

2. Value: the *luminance* or *lightness/darkness* of a color measured against a scale of white to black. Its light-orangeness as compared to its dark-orangeness. How much whiteness or blackness is added to the hue. The light end of the scale is "high," the dark end "low."

3. Chroma: the purity or *brightness* of a color, its *intensity* or *saturation*. The same blue can be pure and vivid, or muted, dirty and greyish. The background against which a color is seen affects its apparent saturation: a bright color surrounded by a duller version of the same color looks saturated, but it is brilliant on a field of its complementary.

Definition and naming of colors Monitor screens which produce color by combining the light from red, green and blue phosphorus, show 16.7 million different hues. (The red, green and blue are each subdivided into 256 shades. So: $256^3 = 16{,}700{,}000$.)

How do we distinguish them all? Giving them names? What precisely is meant by "Toast"? Rye, wholewheat, or pumpernickel? Burned or just light? A more accurate definition has been devised: measuring wavelengths by a *spectrophotometer* (which measures the amount of radiant energy reflected from an object in each wavelength band of the visible spectrum) and matching a color by a *colorimeter*.

The internationally-accepted standard for describing color accurately is the *CIE triangle*. It was established in 1931 by the the Commission Internationale de l'Éclairage (International Commission on Illumination). The *chromaticity diagram* positions colors in relation to their wavelengths which are described in three-digit numbers in nanometers (nm). They define the chromaticity by three values: the intensity of the light (luminance), its hue, and its saturation.

This precise measurement is a dependable definition making it possible to compare colors under any circumstances, no matter what form they may take—additive or subtractive, fresh or faded swatch, natural or artificial, paint, dye, ink, or toner etc.

Perception of color Nothing about color is static. Everything varies, affected by:

1. Lighting conditions Colors change, depending on the brightness of the light. They turn duller and darker as daylight fades into twilight and darkness.

The light under which a white object is looked at affects the kind of whiteness we see:

- Under north light at noon, it would be bluish, because that kind of light is rich in the blue end of the spectrum.
- Under candlelight, it would be yellowish.
- Under an incandescent bulb it would be more reddish because that is rich in the red end of the spectrum.

A practical application: incandescent light emphasizes reds, yellows and greens and so makes vegetables look nice, whereas fluorescent light emphasizes blues and cyans that make vegetables frozen and unappetizing.... what kind of lighting do canny supermarket managers use and where?

Always take the ambient light into account when matching colors. They may match perfectly under one light source, but not under another. The technical term for this phenomenon is *metameric color shift.*

2. The background color The colors in the vicinity affect the way the observed color is perceived. The relationships are vitally important, because colors are relative to each other. For instance:

- Dark colors appear darker on a light background than they do on a darker one.
- Mixing complemetary colors in equal amounts, weakens them and grays them down.
- Complementary colors placed next to each other reinforce each other and if they are of the same value, hurt the eye.

3. The paper The paper is the light-source in printing. Light strikes it and is reflected off its surface to the viewer's eyes. It shines through the three transparent process color inks.

The texture of the surface affects the appearance of the color. The smoother and glossier it is, the brighter and more brilliant the hues look. The same ink printed on a rough texture appears duller because the rough surface scatters the reflected light from the paper, so paling down the appearance of the color. It not only dulls it, but can even alter the appearance of the hue. The smoother and glossier the surface, the more brilliant the effect of the glossy colored inks printed on it. Laser paper is manufactured with a smooth surface specifically to bring out the best detail and quality of laser printing in both the dense blacks and zesty colors by holding the toner particles while withstanding the heat.

The most accurate color reproduction is achieved on paper that reflects light without altering its quality. Such a sheet is said to be *balanced white*. If the paper absorbs some wave lengths more than others, it is unbalanced, and appears to be tinted or *colored*. It will change the effect that process color inks will make. That is why printing with color on colored stock is so unpredictable. Always run tests to make sure your result will be satisfactory.

Reproducing color Mechanical, technical and chemical limitations of the printing process make it impossible to reproduce the full range of colors precisely. The very light and very dark shades are specially difficult.

When transparent inks are overlapped, intermediate colors are produced. Opaque inks do not produce intermediate colors when they overlap, since they do not allow the light to pass through them, but reflect it instead.

Printing pictures in color A *continuous tone* original is an image such as a photograph or painting whose color changes in imperceptibly-small steps from dark to light. To be made printable, the continuous tone must be transformed into a *halftone*. Grey is produced by mixing solid black dots with white reflected from the paper between the dots. The more white (the smaller the dots), the lighter the illusion of grey. The less white, (the bigger the dots), the darker the grey appears. Black has no white showing through, because it is 100% coverage or *solid*.

A *traditional halftone* is made by re-photographing the original through a screen which breaks the image into a dot pattern. The finer the screen (i.e. the greater the screen ruling), the finer the dots, the better the resolution, and therefore the finer the quality of detail. Screen rulings vary from the typical coarse newspaper screen of 85 lpi (or lines per inch—i.e. lines of dots) to 133 lpi used in printing normal magazines. *Process color printing* requires four halftones (one each for ***Y***ellow, ***M***agenta, ***C***yan and blac***K***). Printed on top of each other, they create the impression of colors.

A *computer-created halftone* is not created by varying the size of dots. Instead, it is created by controlling cells, which consist of grids of individual dots that are either on (black) or off (white). The more are "on," the darker does the "gray" appear. At 635 dpi (dots per inch) output, each halftone cell of a 133 lpi (lines per inch) screen consists of 16 pixels (4 x 4) each of which can be either on or off, thus yielding 16 shades of grey. High quality digital halftones should be scanned at double the printed halftone lines-per-inch. For instance at 150 lpi (lines per inch), the scanning resolution should be 300 dpi.

Dithering can produce additional shades, patterns and fills as well as color halftones, where smooth and gradual transition from shade to shade is required. Various formulas for dithering have been developed by software manufacturers.

Color separations The original continuous tone color image is divided into its constituent process colors by scanning. The electronic scanner calculates the percentages of cyan, magenta, yellow and black that each tiny area of the original consists of and creates four separate sheets of film, from which the final printing plates are made.

The four films must be carefully *registered* to fit perfectly. They are made by traditional color separators, service bureaus, or on desktop using programs such as Adobe's Photoshop or Letraset's ColorStudio. Combining several subjects into a single page requires stripping: physically assembling all the bits of film, cutting them, and attaching them to a bearing sheet—for each of the four colors. Obviously, that is an exacting, meticulous (and expensive) hand process, unless it is done by electronic pre-press.

The three kinds of color originals:

- Digitized images and/or video already digitized into pixels (or pels—picture elements). However, their resolution is coarser than that required for good printing.
- Transparencies: continuous tone photographs, easy to scan.
- Reflection copy: color prints of photographs, artists' renderings such as paintings, watercolors etc., which have to be photographed as transparencies in preparation for scanning. The traditional camera-separations are now used for special projects.

Moiré and rosettes Moiré is an unintended pattern when geometric patterns (such as dot-screens of black atop a color) are superimposed on top of each other. It is distracting to see stars where smooth color should be.

Angling the screens properly can avoid it. Traditional four-color process dots are placed at standard angles: cyan at 15°, magenta at 75°, yellow at 0°, and black at 45°. Prepress computers often use algorithms that slightly alter these angles to compensate for the type of laser dot the systems generate. Desktop angles are normally black at 0°, cyan at 30°, magenta at 60°, and yellow at 75°.

Rosettes combine dots of the different process colors in such a way that the human eye is fooled into combining them to "see" them as close to the continuous tone from which the separation was made.

Trapping color Even the highest-quality printing is an inexact process: the moving parts of the press or the motion of the paper itself, cannot be controlled beyond a certain point. Paper stretches, humidity affects shrinkage, speed demands compromises, ink formulations vary, color sequences give differing effects, presses are all different... Though it is amazing how accurate the new processes have become, perfection is not attainable. That is why you sometimes see white gaps between colors that should be touching. To prevent this unsightly unintended sliver, a technique called *trapping* has been evolved. In traditional work, the image is made a fraction larger than the window into which it is to fit, so the contiguous elements actually overlap. In electronic page makeup, the same problem is called *shrink, spread, skinny, fatty, choke.*

Proofing colors Fact: what you see in the original transparency can only be approximated in print. Fact: the colors you see on your screen can not be duplicated in hard copy. There are two common proofing techniques that let you see what you are likely to get:

- Overlay system (such as 3M's Color Key) consists of four acetate sheets, one each for the C, M, Y and K component, overlaid on a white backing sheet.
- Single-laminate sheet (such as duPont's Cromalin, or 3M's Matchprint) combines the four layers into single sheets.

Temper your expectations when checking proofs. A few suggestions:

1. Look for credibility, whether the result makes sense with the effect you are trying to communicate. The best printing is merely an approximation of reality. Perfect match is impossible to achieve.
2. Look for overall color balance.
3. Check for details in the highlight and shadow areas.
4. Evaluate flesh tones for realism.
5. Look for neutral greys and wood tones for realism.
6. Make sure the whites and highlights are sparkly and bright.

Color palettes Four-color separations are made electronically with different techniques. The commonest:

- RGB (red/green/blue),
- HSB (Hue/saturation/brightness, sometimes also called HLS hue/luminance/saturation),
- CMYK (cyan/magenta/yellow/black) and
- Palette color (a fixed library of colors, usually 256).

RGB and HSB are generally used for scanned images since scanners capture information in RGB format. However, final output must be in CMYK to make it printable. Conversion is necessary. But the programs are often not compatible resulting in confusion as well as disappointment. Use CMYK specifications wherever possible. All you can do with scanned images is hope for the best.

Matching colors Do not expect the additive colors on screen to be matched precisely by the subtractive colors in print. The two modalities may look similar but they are not the same, and despite efforts in software-calculations, they can never be identical. Inaccuracy in calibration, differing lighting conditions and other uncontrollable unpredictable problems prevent it.

The screen is bound to look brighter because it is back-lit, so the colors cannot help but sparkle more vividly. Besides, the printing process itself is incapable of reproducing the subtleties the eye can discern in the original version of the subject. Nor can its infinite variables such as humidity, paper surface absorptivity, variety of presses or copiers etc etc be controlled. That is why sensible compromise is required.

Tint-builds vs PMS colors There is a big difference between flat color *(spot color, highlight color, second color)* and four-color process. Flat color is an ink or toner using specially-mixed hues to produce one specific color, not process colors. That is the kind of precisely matched color needed in logos, for instance, where exact color matching is often crucial to the corporate identity program.

Such mixed-ink colors were the foundation for the PMS, Pantone Matching System®. Its formulas for proprietary ink mixtures were coordinated with colored papers, markers, overlay films, etc., and gained worldwide acceptance as a dependable means of communication about color.

However, PMS colors are not the same as CMYK colors. PMS colors must be transformed into CMYK tint builds. Matching a color by tint build out of percentages of the four process colors (cyan, magenta, yellow, plus black) is possible. However, such simulation cannot be absolutely accurate, especially in the lighter or darker hues, nor can the color effect ever be as intense or as vivid. The brighter and cleaner the color, the more difficult does it become to match it in tint builds. The dirtier the color, the easier it is to match.

To ensure perfect match, a mixed ink (specified as a PMS color or any other commercially available system) has to be used on a separate cylinder on press. Obviously, a five-color press is needed (one with five or more cylinders or "units". One each for the four process colors plus the fifth for the matched color).

The three major process-color matching systems that are available and are supported by graphic programs are Trumatch and Focoltone, which are exclusively 4-color systems, and Pantone, which also makes a 4-color guide. They all provide fan-shaped color-finders which show the available colors. Don't be sorry that you can't have all the millions of hues your software is capable of making. The thousands that Trumatch, Focoltone, and Pantone give you are ample to work with. What's more, you can be sure that you'll get what you specify—with luck.

Trumatch organizes over 2000 colors by hue, saturation and brightness in a user-friendly and intuitive system: you can easily find colors that bear close family relationship—brighter or duller, lighter or darker. The differences between Trumatch colors are logical, because formulations are based on accurate proportions in 1% increments. Colors are shown on both coated and uncoated papers. The differences are serious.

Focoltone shows 763 standard colors using 5% screens along more printing-oriented lines. Each starting color made up of 4-color tints is analyzed in groupings that subtract a process color layer. Thus you see four 3-color combinations, six 2-color combinations and the four single CMYK layers. Similar colors can be several groups apart, so it is more difficult to compare them to each other than in Trumatch.

Pantone organizes the fanguide into 2-color combinations with their shades, followed by 3-color and 4-color combinations, with the main color at the top and examples of decreased saturation and brightness below. Similar colors are not necessarily next to each other. The swatch book is on coated stock only, but shows 3000 colors.

If you have no process color guide (which you should invest in), you can specify colors according to process color charts you get from your printer. Find the swatch you like, then specify the percentages of CMYK of which it is built.

30

This type is easily legible on a pale screen, but the darker the tint, the more uncomfortable does reading become. If the background is too dark, few will bother to read the text at all.

70

This type is easily legible on a pale screen, but the darker the tint, the more uncomfortable does reading become. If the background is too dark, few will bother to read the text at all.

90

This type is easily legible on a pale screen, but the darker the tint, the more uncomfortable does reading become. If the background is too dark, few will bother to read the text at all.

20

This type is easily legible on a pale screen, but the darker the tint, the more uncomfortable does reading become. If the background is too dark, few will bother to read the text at all.

10

This type is easily legible on a pale screen, but the darker the tint, the more uncomfortable does reading become. If the background is too dark, few will bother to read the text at all.

60

This type is easily legible on a pale screen, but the darker the tint, the more uncomfortable does reading become. If the background is too dark, few will bother to read the text at all.

50

This type is easily legible on a pale screen, but the darker the tint, the more uncomfortable does reading become. If the background is too dark, few will bother to read the text at all.

100

This type is easily legible on a pale screen, but the darker the tint, the more uncomfortable does reading become. If the background is too dark, few will bother to read the text at all.

80

This type is easily legible on a pale screen, but the darker the tint, the more uncomfortable does reading become. If the background is too dark, few will bother to read the text at all.

40

This type is easily legible on a pale screen, but the darker the tint, the more uncomfortable does reading become. If the background is too dark, few will bother to read the text at all.

Use it up, wear it out;
Make it do, or do without 60

Use it up, wear it out;
Make it do, or do without 20

Use it up, wear it out;
Make it do, or do without 40

Use it up, wear it out;
Make it do, or do without 30

Use it up, wear it out;
Make it do, or do without 50

Use it up, wear it out;
Make it do, or do without 10

Use it up, wear it out;
Make it do, or do without 70

The impossible takes a little longer

The impossible takes a little longer

The impossible takes a **little** longer

The impossible takes a little longer

The impossible takes a little longer

The impossible takes a **little** longer

The impossible takes a little longer

The impossible takes a little longer

The impossible takes a **little** longer

When graphic design is considered as an end in itself and is done for its own sake, then it is terrifying indeed, for its validity depends entirely on one's subjective "liking," and "liking" is a quality no one can define and few can agree about. All anyone can do is to feel insecure about it and defend one's arbitrary position. Furthermore, such an approach to design is nothing but a quest for superficial beauty: making a publication look good and pleasing to the eye. It is, of course, possible to develop such cosmetic gloss on any product, but that approach was nailed down forever by Oscar Wilde when he referred to the dead fish in the moonlight: "It glistens, but it stinks." When graphic design is regarded as a means to an end, then it is no longer self-centered art-for-art's sake. That is a very different kettle of fish that smells delicious. As such, it becomes accessible to anyone: those who originate the product as well as those who receive it.

When graphic design is considered as an end in itself and is done for its own sake, then it is terrifying indeed, for its validity depends entirely on one's subjective "liking," and "liking" is a quality no one can define and few can agree about. All anyone can do is to feel insecure about it and defend one's arbitrary position. Furthermore, such an approach to design is nothing but a quest for superficial beauty: making a publication look good and pleasing to the eye. It is, of course, possible to develop such cosmetic gloss on any product, but that approach was nailed down forever by Oscar Wilde when he referred to the dead fish in the moonlight: "It glistens, but it stinks." When graphic design is regarded as a means to an end, then it is no longer self-centered art-for-art's sake. That is a very different kettle of fish that smells delicious. As such, it becomes accessible to anyone: those who originate the product as well as those who receive it.

When graphic design is considered as an end in itself and is done for its own sake, then it is terrifying indeed, for its validity depends entirely on one's subjective "liking," and "liking" is a quality no one can define and few can agree about. All anyone can do is to feel insecure about it and defend one's arbitrary position. Furthermore, such an approach to design is nothing but a quest for superficial beauty: making a publication look good and pleasing to the eye. It is, of course, possible to develop such cosmetic gloss on any product, but that approach was nailed down forever by Oscar Wilde when he referred to the dead fish in the moonlight: "It glistens, but it stinks." When graphic design is regarded as a means to an end, then it is no longer self-centered art-for-art's sake. That is a very different kettle of fish that smells delicious. As such, it becomes accessible to anyone: those who originate the product as well as those who receive it.